CULTURAL CHANGE *and*
ORD`▪`

STANDARD LOAN

SOCIOLOGY *and* **SOCIAL CHANGE**

Series Editors: *Alan* **Warde,** *Nick* **Crossley, University of Manchester**

Published titles

Amanda **Coffey – Education** *and* **Social Change**
Allison **Cavanagh – Sociology in the Age of the Internet**
Nick **Crossley – Reflexive Embodiment in Contemporary Society**
Sara **Delamont – Changing Women, Unchanged Men?**
Andy **Furlong** *and Fred* **Cartmel – Young People** *and* **Social Change** (second edition)
Gail **Hawkes –** *A* **Sociology** *of* **Sex** *and* **Sexuality**
Colin **Hay – Re-stating Social** *and* **Political Change**
Máirtín **Mac an Ghaill – Contemporary Racisms** *and* **Ethnicities**
Mike **Savage – Class Analysis** *and* **Social Transformation**

Cultural Change *and* Ordinary Life

Brian **Longhurst**

Open University Press

Open University Press
McGraw-Hill Education
McGraw-Hill House
Shoppenhangers Road
Maidenhead
Berkshire
England
SL6 2QL

email: enquiries@openup.co.uk
world wide web: www.openup.co.uk

and Two Penn Plaza, New York, NY 10121–2289, USA

First published 2007

Copyright © Brian Longhurst 2007

A catalogue record of this book is available from the British Library

ISBN13: 978 0 335 22187 5 (pb)   978 0 335 22188 2 (hb)
ISBN10: 0 335 22187 4 (pb)   0 335 22188 2 (hb)

Library of Congress Cataloging-in-Publication Data
CIP data applied for

Typeset by RefineCatch Limited, Bungay, Suffolk
Printed in Poland by OZGraf S.A.
www.polskabook.pl

The *McGraw·Hill* Companies

Contents

Acknowledgements   vii

1   Introduction   1

2   Concepts *and* **theories** *of* **everyday** *and* **ordinary life**   7
    The everyday   8
    Ordinary life   12
    Music, sound and ordinary life   16
    Conclusion   20

3   Changing ordinary life   22
    Globalizing and hybridizing   22
    Modernity, fragmentation and personal choice   25
    Spectacularizing and performing   28
    Enthusing   30
    Conclusion   34

4   Understanding *and* **theorizing cultural change**   35
    Spectacle, performance and performativity   35
    Audience positions   42
    Research questions   44
    Conclusion   48

5   Globalizing, hybridizing *and* **localizing: processes** *of*
    elective belonging   49
    Belonging   49
    Globalizing   51
    Scenes   52
    Scene, performing, audiencing and elective belonging   58
    Conclusion   61

6   Imagining, performing *and* **identifying: class, identity** *and* **culture** 62
    Class, culture and identity: a new agenda   63

Inscription, exchange, value and perspective   69
Morality, evaluation and ordinary life   71
Conclusion   73

7   Distinguishing *and* connecting 1: capitals *and the* use *of* time   74
Time use   75
Social capital in Britain   81
Class and education: economic, cultural and social resources   85
Conclusion   88

8   Distinguishing *and* connecting 2: *the* omnivore thesis   90
The omnivore thesis: early statements and key themes   92
The omnivore thesis: wider applications and development of
explanations   97
Cultural taste: qualitative consideration and modes of speech   100
Conclusion   102

9   Enthusing   104
Processes of reception and sport   105
Theories of fandom   110
Place, space and the extended audience   115
Enthusing: diffusion and the self   117

10   Conclusions   119

References   125
Index   133

Acknowledgements

This book is the product of a number of years' work. In many respects, it represents a summary of where I have reached in a 'project' that has been going on for much of my academic life. During that period, I have engaged in funded research and worked with colleagues who have influenced my thinking in many ways.

First, I want to pay credit to the PhD students with whom I have worked over the years: Jason Rutter, Eamonn Carrabine, Gaynor Bagnall, Tony Kearon, Garry Crawford, Dan Laughey, Annemarie Money, Kath O'Connor, David Redfern, Sylvia Hayes and Danijela Bogdanovic. They have all helped me crystallize my ideas and challenged me to think them through. Second, I have worked on funded research projects that exposed me to different ideas and approaches. These are a study of middle-class lifestyles (ESRC, *Lifestyles and Social Integration: A Study of Middle Class Culture in Manchester*) with Gaynor Bagnall and Mike Savage; a project on young people and popular music (funded by Manchester Airport, *Music, Identity and Lifestyle in Contemporary Manchester*) with Eamonn Carrabine; work on hearing, noise and sound (EPSRC, *Hearing Loss in the Built Environment: The Experience of Elderly People*) with Bill Davies, Trevor Cox, Tony Kearon and Clare Webb; and research on social networks and political activism (ESRC, *Social Capital and Social Networks: The Careers of Political Activists*) with Mike Savage, Alan Warde, Mark Tomlinson, Gindo Tampubolon and Kath Ray. All these projects have had major effects on the ideas in this book and I want to thank my colleagues and, of course, those who funded the research. Third, there are my colleagues in Sociology at the University of Salford who have listened to me and provided many insights. Thanks are due, in particular, to Rob Flynn and Greg Smith for these things and the support and advice during my period as Head of the School of English, Sociology, Politics and Contemporary History. Karl Dayson has helped me think through ideas concerning social capital. Fourth, there are those colleagues from other universities who have helped develop the ideas here. Foremost here I want to thank (again) Nick Abercrombie for his insight, wisdom and very helpful comments on the first draft of this book. Conversations with David Hesmondhalgh, Nick Couldry and Pete Peterson have all affected the approach here, as has the reading of their books and articles.

My intellectual debts to Mike Savage, Alan Warde, Gaynor Bagnall and Eamonn Carrabine go beyond the work already mentioned in many ways. Alan's insightful comments on the first draft of this book have helped me refine and improve the ideas in a number of ways. In addition, the discussion with many colleagues at seminars and conferences has had a significant input. Finally, my thanks to the School of English, Sociology, Politics and Contemporary History and the Faculty of Arts, Media and Social Sciences at the University of Salford for allowing me study leave in the period before taking over as Dean so that I could work on this book. Special thanks here to Jackie Flynn and Richard Towell for the space and advice in the 'lead in' and since.

This book seeks to understand 'ordinary' life. My own ordinary life informs that understanding. Thanks go again to Mum and Dad for their interest and support. Above all, most thanks go to Bernadette, James and Tim. I can never put into words the extent of my debts and feelings to you all. But you make the ordinary extraordinary in more ways than I can capture.

1 Introduction

There are many books that address the nature of everyday life and even more that examine cultural change and the media.[1] This book is about all three topics. It seeks to offer a new approach to the understanding of these inter-related themes. In this introduction, I offer some background that points up the need for the sort of book that this is. This offers an initial consideration of the main themes that I will subsequently explore. The second part of the introduction details the content of the chapters that follow.

A key theme of this book is that the increased importance of media of communication has had a significant effect on the nature of ordinary life in a contemporary consumerist capitalist society such as that in the UK. This statement of theme immediately introduces three significant questions. First, what is meant by increased importance? Second, what are media of communication? And, third, what is meant by ordinary life? I offer now some initial clarification of my understanding of these issues, before turning to some other points of introductory significance.

In my view, the idea that media are becoming of increased importance has often been misunderstood. To be clear, I will not seek to argue (along the lines of some representations of the work of Jean Baudrillard) that society has become equivalent to media life. While the 'hype' surrounding such 'post-modern' ideas often has a role in pointing up how ubiquitous the media have become, it rapidly becomes subject to diminishing returns. Social life and cultural life are not the same as media life. If such a strong argument for the significance of the media is to be rejected, as missing the point that many events happen outwith the media, then it also seems important to recognize that society and culture have been changed quite fundamentally by the availability of a range of media as resources for the conduct of everyday life. Data and theories that support this contention will be considered as this book progresses.

At the moment consider the following differences over 50 years. I write as a member of the first British TV generation (I was born in 1956 – the year after commercial TV started) in that I can't remember life before TV. In my early life, I went to the cinema when it still showed newsreels, when two feature films were on the bill and when the national anthem was played at the end of the night (some people still stood up). However, as a child in cosmo-politan, 'glocalizing' south London (in Brixton) in the 1960s, the only TV in the house was black and white and we could receive two channels (the Scottish part of my family had only recently received commercial TV). Music came on 45rpm, 33^1/$_3$ 'long players' (as a big investment) and the 45rpm EP (extended play). Tape recorders were reel to reel on big boxes. Radio was being trans-formed due to the offshore pirates, but in a way that actually retained much of the structure of BBC stations that had been existence for many years. Portable transistor radios were now common, but still pretty new. Books came mainly through borrowing from the local public library and magazines were passed around family and friends. The daily newspaper was the *Daily Sketch* and my father would bring in the London *Evening News* from work (there were still two London evening newspapers). We had one of the first telephones in the street, partly to keep in contact with family in Scotland (which involved placing a call with the operator until the late 1960s), but the device was also a resource for neighbours, who would come round to use the telephone and for whom friends and family would call. Letters and parcels were the main means of communication outside face-to-face talk.

I now live in a 'gentrified' village north of Manchester in the north-west of England. Television is digital and involves many channels (even without a subscription to Sky), including seven BBC channels. The TV will also provide numerous radio channels. There are five TVs in the house (more than there are people). The cinema usually involves driving to a local multiplex, which is surrounded by restaurants, bars, a gym, and so on. The DVD player is con-nected to the TV and while the VCRs (three) are still used, the next generations of home recording are only around the corner. Music mainly comes on CD and there are many shelves of them. iPods are recent acquisitions and are used increasingly frequently. There are two computers in the house and four lap-tops come in and out. These provide web and email contact. There are two telephone landlines and four mobile phones and I can easily dial across the world and send texts. There are two computer game consoles. Books are pur-chased and then often passed on or sent to charity stores as there is not enough space for them. The daily newspaper is *The Guardian* and the local evening newspaper is only purchased on special occasions. Various magazines are purchased and recycled.

It is possible to read these last two paragraphs as a narrative of upward social mobility to a professional position and they contain many individual nuances. However, despite these caveats, the experience condenses, I think, something of what I mean by the idea that the media are of increased import-ance. There is, on one level, more of them (although note that there are fewer newspapers and certainly fewer deliveries and collections of the post) and they allow us access to more things and information. I am well aware that these media resources are distributed unequally across our society (as are nearly all resources and opportunities) in a structured way. However, despite the depth of my own resources, many with less income also have a significant range of media resources. It is inconceivable to me that this level of shift does not have implications for our ways of life, but they do not, to repeat, erase other aspects of our lives. In one respect, then, this book is about the relationship between media and other parts of our lives. As might be suggested by the content of those two paragraphs, it is possible that while my media life has become more resourced, my locality of residence is far less diverse and my face-to-face contact will primarily be with other white middle-class people, in great contrast to my experiences of south London of the 1960s and 1970s when I was growing up. This suggests that there are some complex interactions between living spaces and media lives.

In addition, I have mentioned family and work. I am firmly of the view that as well as considering residence and media, patterns of interaction among family (and friends) and relationships to work also have to be considered alongside media interactions and this book will have this as a focus. My point is that media resources have expanded greatly and that to understand our culture we need to see researching and understanding this as a key aim. Common ways of thinking of this have involved ideas that society is media saturated or media drenched. I prefer to work with the latter term, as the former perhaps suggests that no more can be added and I do not think that we have reached the end point of media development. Such media drenching has a range of implications for our lives. I have considered some aspects of the implications of this process in earlier work (Abercrombie and Longhurst 1998) and will use this as a base in some of the subsequent discussion.

Part of how I define the media has also been communicated by the earlier brief characterization of media availability. I will adopt a broad definition of what is meant by media. One of the problems with the history of the study of the media is that it has tended to be skewed by most attention to film and television. While understandable on a number of levels – including the popularity of both of these forms as mass entertainment – this has tended to lead to other media becoming the 'poor' relations. However, this is now changing at a rapid pace, as the literatures on other media, including radio as well as 'new' media, develop. The book will therefore seek to take into account these developments and not to become a study of television. Another reason for this is that admirable theoretical and empirical studies of TV and everyday life already exist (for example, Lembo 2000; Silverstone 1994). While I will not be able to cover all media in anything like great depth, I do think that it is important to recognize the range of media that are potentially significant in ordinary life. These include mobile phones, mp3 players, and so on. One consequence of this attention to a range of media will be that I want to include and therefore value the way in which sound is significant in ordinary life. There still tends to be a prime focus on the visual media in media studies. Again, while this is understandable, it is limiting, especially as media 'converge' technologically.

The third question introduced earlier was the *nature of ordinary life*. I will examine in more detail the reasons for my terminology here in Chapter 2. There I will consider the main parameters of extant theories of everyday life and distinguish my approach from them. I will do this in accord with some of the arguments outlined in previous work on audiences, but will introduce some further aspects. In short, I will suggest that the idea of ordinary life is sociologically significant in illuminating how life is lived out. One of the great interventions of cultural studies in its earliest formulations was to point the way in which academic attention should be paid to how culture is 'lived'. Some of the ways in which this lead to the prioritization of the idea of 'experience' became somewhat problematic as this literature developed.[2] However, I will maintain that attention to the lived means that sociology, cultural and media studies can detail and explain key aspects of social and cultural life. For this to happen it is necessary to draw on the resource of key aspects of contemporary social and cultural theory; in particular, I will argue those that address ideas of performance and audiences are of greatest significance. Using these resources will lead me to be critical of many of those accounts of everyday life that either work on the premise that everyday life is in principle compromised or inauthentic or that everyday life involves resistance to a dominant power structure. Following and expanding on Silverstone (1994), especially via some of the literature on music and sound, I will offer an alternative account.

There is another sub-theme that influences my attention to ordinary life. I seek to explore the value of the living out of ordinary life, not as resistant to centralized or fragmented power but as providing the meanings and routines that enable people to experience the everyday joys and pleasures (to be sure there are many drawbacks as well) of simply going about their lives. I think that despite some of its many difficulties, some of which will be considered in this book, the seminal work of Putnam (e.g. 2000) on social capital (see Chapter 3) captures something of what I feel in this respect. Moreover, sociology and cultural studies have not paid sufficient attention to these concrete pleasures of ordinary life. The use of ordinary therefore has some measure of polemic behind it. I write not as a critic of everyday life or a celebrant of its resistive qualities, but as an analyst of the sometimes extraordinary qualities of the ordinary lives of people living in a society such as ours.

I have other views that influence the way that this book has been put together. Doubtless these will seem idiosyncratic in many respects, but part of my desire here is to shift some literatures that seem rather too stuck in modes of 'normal science' at present. First, I want to suggest that reconciliations between aspects of what might be seen as more 'orthodox' sociology and political science and media and cultural studies would be beneficial. Aspects of sociology's findings on how people use their time and political science's analysis of participation in civic activities and trust can be brought to bear on media and cultural studies' research on audiences and fans. This I will maintain can be of mutual benefit. Second, and partly because of these disciplinary boundaries, some of the work on culture in North American sociology has been relatively poorly integrated with cultural and media studies. While only aspects of this work will be drawn on in this book, I will address at several points issues of how work on cultural taste needs to be considered alongside cutting-edge audience studies. The idea of social capital is but one arena where these different strands can be brought together profitably. Third, I seek to emphasize and try to understand further the living out of social and cultural change. There have been many accounts that offer grand narratives of such change: for example, arguments about late modernity and postmodernity (which have become unfashionable rather too quickly in my view; see Matthewman and Hoey 2006); globalization/hybridization; and hypermodernity. Such accounts offer a range of suggestive tools, especially I will argue around ideas of how belonging is constituted in a society like that in the contemporary UK.

On the basis of a range of resources, the book will offer a new way of understanding the processes of ordinary life. My argument, which develops as the book progresses, so therefore to summarize, consists of the following claims:

- Ordinary life is important, is often theorized inadequately in the context of theories that are of little contemporary use in understanding complex social changes and is itself changing.
- Ordinary life is media drenched and is increasingly constituted around mediatized processes, but is not the same as media life.
- Ordinary life needs to be understood in the context of key contexualizing processes of social and cultural change: globalizing/hybridizing; fragmenting; spectacularization and performing; and enthusing.
- Ordinary life should be conceptualized as involving the interaction between audience and performance processes.
- Through these processes of audiencing and performing, three other rather general processes are played and lived out: belonging, distinguishing and individualizing.
- That important light has been shed on these processes by research on social class and culture and that given that class has often been thought to be an outdated concept, this is worthy of sustained attention.
- In summary, my argument is that while social and cultural life is, as a consequence of media drenching becoming increasingly audienced and performed, these processes of audiencing and performing involve people in forging new ways of belonging that seek, as well as making them feel like some people (to belong), to also distinguish them from others and to make them feel that are individuals and not just like everyone else.

At the moment this is only a statement of the argument, which I will build up over the course of the pages that follow. The book is structured as follows. The next chapter will review the history and current state of theorizing of the idea of everyday life. I will offer a pretty brisk overview of these theories and, in accord with the approach already articulated, offer some reasons as to why I think this literature, despite its many insights that are mobilized at points, does not offer a way forward for the enterprise of this book. Second, again building on some extant work on the idea of ordinariness, I develop the argument for the use of this idea to theorize the way in which life is lived. A third significant component of this chapter is to argue for the significance of sound and music in everyday life.

Chapter 3 reviews some of the key changes that have affected ordinary life. This will provide a base for some of the more detailed discussion in subsequent chapters. Four key areas of social and cultural change are considered and specific instances of the processes as they are affecting life in the UK will be examined. This is significant as it deepens the argument about why a new understanding of ordinary life is necessary. First, I will consider the impact of processes of globalization and hybridization, where forms of mobility are of increased significance. Second, I will discuss theories that suggest that culture is subject to processes of fragmentation. Until the mid- to late 1990s there was a tendency to group these accounts under the idea of 'postmodernism' or 'postmodernity'; while these labels have increasingly fallen into disuse, the processes that were captured by them are still subject to theorization and significantly empirical research. Thus, I will argue that the 'omnivore' thesis is in an important sense an empirical investigation of the fragmentation thesis. Third, there are a number of arguments that suggest that ordinary life has become more organized around ideas of spectacle and performance. We display more and we act more for the camera. Fourth, I will consider the evidence about the way in which attachment to voluntary associations and 'fan'-like processes has impacted on ordinary life. This will involve an initial consideration of the idea of social capital. Each of these areas will be considered through a case study example.

Having reviewed these changes and theories, Chapter 4 will argue for a particular way of understanding the processes involved. This will start from ideas of the way in which audiences are changing and further develop considerations of performance and spectacle. Again drawing on empirical research, it will further exemplify some of the key anchoring points of ordinary life. In a number of senses Chapters 2 to 4 set the ground for further and deeper examination of the issues and evidence in the rest of the book. Chapter 5 focuses on ideas of globalizing, hybridizing and localizing. This is followed by a chapter that looks at arguments about how identities and the sense of the self are produced in a society such as we find in the UK to day. This is followed by two chapters that analyse processes by which people distinguish themselves from others, as well as how they reconnect to each other. Chapter 7 will start from the ideas of Pierre Bourdieu and consider the work that has been done on class (and increasingly gender) using his ideas of the relationships between different forms of capital. Chapter 8 examines the omnivore thesis in some depth. Chapter 9 will consider processes of I what I propose to call enthusing – how people form attachments to a range of activities in civil society around clubs, fanlike attachments to TV programmes, music, and so on. This will point up some of the 'extraordinary' moments of ordinary life. In the conclusion to the book, I will show, as clearly as I can, how the different aspects of the argument relate to one another.

Notes

1 In this introduction, I have kept references to a readable minimum for ease of exposition. As the topics are considered at further length in the main body of the book, appropriate references are provided.
2 As in the work of Raymond Williams.

2 Concepts *and* theories *of* everyday *and* ordinary life

As I show later, the concept of everyday life has been central to a range of theoretical developments in sociology, cultural and media studies. I begin this chapter with a succinct overview of these theories. My reasons for brevity are twofold. First, given that extensive reviews of the concept of everyday life already exist (see for example, Gardiner 2000; Highmore 2002), it would seem redundant to spend extensive space in this book repeating what has been done elsewhere. Second, and far more importantly, my argument will be that much of this literature is actually unhelpful for the project of this book. Bennett and Silva (2004) argue in a similar vein, when in discussion of the work of Crook (1998) who they suggest 'proposes that it might be better to jettison the concept of the everyday altogether' (p. 3), they advance the view that:

> To the contrary, the categories of the everyday and everyday life remain valuable and valid in their references to the ordinary and mundane, but only provided that these categories are emptied out of much of their earlier theoretical and political content.

> (Bennett and Silva 2004: 4)

My argument will be that if we are to focus on the ordinary and the mundane, which I suggest is precisely what should be done, and how these are being transformed in contemporary society, then it is best to take a leap and call this ordinary life. This will be my contention. Thus, the overview of everyday life theory will involve the pulling out of the key specific processes of everyday life accounts that are best thought of as ordinary and mundane.

This leads logically to the second part of the chapter, which examines the idea of the ordinary more carefully. I begin from the still significant work of Raymond Williams (1989) on this topic, but suggest some refinements of his approach. One important source for this revision is the work of Nick Couldry (2000a), but I will also draw on other sources to ground this discussion. The final part of the chapter seeks to show how this idea of ordinary life might begin to work through looking at the way in which music and sound are threaded through it. Two key sources are mobilized here from the work of Michael Bull (2000) and Tia DeNora (2000). A further point of this aspect of the discussion is to suggest that music and sound have tended to be underplayed in previous discussions of everyday life and that indeed this is one of the reasons for their deficiencies (see also Hesmondhalgh 2002).

The everyday

In his book, *Television and Everyday Life*, Silverstone (1994) offers a succinct and pointed discussion of theories of everyday life. In suggesting that it is important to show how television is implicated in the flow and processes of everyday life, Silverstone argues that previous theories of everyday life with particular reference to media fall into two broad camps, which actually share a number of assumptions. The first approach is that associated with a range of Marxist writers who, from the standpoint of arguing for a fundamental change in economic, political and social life, offer a critique of the way in which life is lived in societies where human beings are alienated due to the way in which they are estranged from the products of their labour and the fundamental tenets of what it is to be human. Thus in Silverstone's words such accounts are critical of everyday life in capitalist societies as 'a real need falsely met' (p. 162). A critical point is that human beings have real needs for sociability, entertainment, interaction, and so on, but these are met and organized by the institutions of capitalism, such as the entertainment corporations that produce 'false' wants and that do not fundamentally satisfy 'real' human needs. In general terms, the problems with such arguments are well known. Most significantly, it is actually difficult to specify what real human needs might be in the abstract beyond the most basic for human sustenance, warmth and reproduction. This means that the critique of everyday life is carried in the name of an account or theory of everyday life that can only be ultimately that which the theorist has constructed. While this may have polemical and political import, it skews social and cultural understanding fundamentally from the beginning. On this basis, I suggest that these sorts of account should and must be rejected. Of course, this does not mean that other Marxist-derived insights concerning, for example, economic exploitation, social and cultural exclusion and social conflict should also be rejected. Rather the principle of analysis should be that the forms of everyday life that may be based on such arrangements should not *a priori* be subject to critique because they are so based.

The second version of everyday life that Silverstone identifies, while it shares a number of premises with the critical Marxist approach such as an argument that suggests that everyday life rests on structures that are fundamentally exploitative, comes to a different account. It focuses on the way in which everyday life contains a range of activity that is resisting or opposing the forms of domination that fundamentally structure everyday life. Silverstone argues that this sort of approach that has been appropriated from the work of de Certeau was fed into the study of media and especially television by Fiske, who emphasized the way in which resistant or active audiences were able to oppose the dominant messages sewn into the media texts promulgated by media corporations.

In many ways therefore, theories of everyday life, that have been based on some Marxist premises and which have been influential in media and cultural studies, resemble what has been called the incorporation/resistance paradigm (IRP) for the study of media audiences. In our book (Abercrombie and Longhurst 1998: 15) on audiences, we argued, therefore, that:

> The Incorporation/Resistance paradigm (IRP henceforth) defines the *problem* of audience research as whether audience members are incorporated into the dominant ideology by their participation in media activity or whether, to the contrary, they are resistant to that incorporation.

Theories of everyday life, in Silverstone's account, are much the same. One of the many problems with the account of everyday life as resistant or oppositional is that it works with an idea of power that is based on a unified dominant structure. Part of our argument in the audiences book was that once power was conceptualized in a different (classically Foucauldian) way – as for example fragmented and operating in micro-contexts to produce forms of practice and discourse – such an account of audiences and indeed everyday life could not be sustained, as it made it impossible to determine what was meant by resistance and opposition (and indeed incorporation).

Silverstone offers another theory of everyday life that he argues can overcome the deficiencies of those that have been discussed so far. This builds on his account of how television is involved as a transitional object in the building of human subjectivity in advanced capitalist countries, as well as ideas of how television is a part of the management of ontological security. Silverstone is indebted to the social theory of Giddens, especially his theory of structuration. Insofar as this stresses the process-like nature of everyday life and that human beings are both subject to structural constraint and able to transform and activity engage in everyday lives, then it is an emphasis that I will follow. On these psychological and sociological foundations, Silverstone offers the following formulation:

> Our everyday lives are the expression, in their taken-for-grantedness, as well as (in popular culture) their self consciousness, of our capacity to hold a line against the generalised anxiety and the threat of chaos that in a *sine qua non* of social life. In this sense everyday life is a continuous achievement (Garkinkel, 1967; Goffman, 1969) more or less ritualised, more or less taken for granted, more or less fragile, in the face of the unknown, the unexpected or the catastrophic.
>
> (1994: 165)

This is a significant emphasis, in that it offers a starting point for an attention to ordinary life that emphasizes everyday social interaction and its dynamics, offering to use some emphases from interactionist sociology. However, it does not take on some of the concerns that I wish to consider in this book, such as social change, cultural dynamism and how life is lived out in a consumerist society. Thus, Silverstone takes me only partly to where I want to be in this chapter. To take the argument forward it is necessary first to address some aspects of the literature introduced by the quotation from Silverstone: interactionist sociology.

As with those theories of everyday life that have been based on Marxist premises that have been briefly considered so far, interactionist sociology (considered in the broadest sense) has had much to say on the topic of everyday life – indeed the topic has been part of sociology since its classical period, especially in the work of Simmel (see, for example, Highmore 2002: 33–44). Particularly important in the theorization of everyday life has been the work of Goffman (1969, 1974), especially via his emphasis on the idea of the way in which everyday life consists of forms of performance. This seminal idea will be developed in various ways during the course of the discussion in this book. An important debt to this analysis has already been paid in earlier work on audiences (Abercrombie and Longhurst 1998: 74), where we suggested that Goffman's work 'indicates that performance is entirely pervasive in everyday life and practically constitutive of it' (p. 74). While this therefore will be an important influence on the account here, the critical points made in the earlier work still stand. The argument that we made was our view of contemporary audiences, based on the specificity of the nature of contemporary performance, rather than its essential character as part of the human condition. In a connected way, the key reason for this specificity 'is that the media of mass communications provide an important resource for everyday performance' (Abercrombie and Longhurst 1998: 74).

While the emphasis on ethnography that has been a key part of the interactionist sociology tradition is one that must be followed, the key issue for the tradition for the argument that I make here is specificity and, in particular, the way in which the media drenching identified in the Introduction is progressing at some pace. Thus, as with the quasi-Marxist tradition there are problems here of how to deal with social and cultural change, the dynamic modes of interaction based on new and more extensive forms of mobility, and the way in which ordinary life is lived out – rather than the formal categories of everyday life. The role of the media is insufficiently emphasized.

In broad terms, the terrain that has been discussed here so far has been captured in a similar way in the work of Bennett and Watson (2002a), who discuss the European critical Marxist tradition, the North American tradition from the Chicago School to Goffman and Garfinkel. They go on to consider work in the British cultural studies tradition, which I discuss at further length later. Three other traditions, which have degrees of overlap, should also be recognized: the surrealist critique of everyday life; the attempt to capture everyday life in documentary projects like Mass Observation and the feminist critique of everyday life.

The project of surrealism has been seen by a number of commentators as offering resources for the social and cultural analysis and critique of everyday life. The tradition connects with Marxism and Mass Observation, but also feeds into the activities of later art/political movements such as situationism. Thus, Gardiner (2000) points out that while the Dada/situationist movement was not that influential in its own period on politics, it did have later effects on social and cultural theory and other movements. In particular, its emphasis on the role of art in everyday life has been an important influence on understandings of consumer practices as they become more aetheticized. Likewise, Highmore (2002) points to the influence of surrealism on social and cultural theory in general and particularly on that of Walter Benjamin. Another key influence of this tradition, which is shown well by Highmore, is on the documentary tradition of Mass Observation.

In Highmore's account, Mass Observation 'combines the legacy of Surrealism with an ethnographic approach to everyday life' (2002: 74). In an engaging discussion of the approach, Highmore brings out the tensions that were involved:

> From the start, Mass-Observation can be seen as characterized by tensions and conflicts, both across its various practices and between the perspectives of those involved in the project. Most of these tensions are not only productive for the project, but an inevitable and necessary response to its initial conception. Emerging as it does on the fault-line between science and art, objectivity and subjectivity, rationalism and irrationalism, there is something necessarily unstable about the project. While attempts for accounting for Mass-Observation often end up privileging one side of this divide at the expense of the other, the difficulty of maintaining the precarious balance of its conflicting aims is often evidenced in the work of those who participated in it.
>
> (Highmore 2002: 77)

Conceptualizing Mass Observation in this fashion reinforces the point that the mundane and the ordinary can be conceptualized and studied in ways that respect the meaningfulness of artistic production and consumption in everyday life. This is of some significance for the overall argument of this book. The final broad area that has been of significance in the study of everyday life has come from the emphasis of feminist writers and related discussion of gender. On the one hand, this is represented by the theoretical interventions of writers such as Dorothy E. Smith (e.g. 1987), as discussed insightfully by Gardiner (2000: 180–206) and, on the other, the emphasis on the challenge represented by feminist writers to 'the negative values that are often associated with the distinctive temporal rhythms of everyday life in its routine and repetitive aspects, contending that these derive from a masculine preference for linear and progressive constructions of time' (Bennett and Watson 2002a: xviii).

At this point, it can initially be seen that these theories of everyday life might be applied across a range of different aspects of everyday life that might almost be a description of everyday life itself. Thus, Bennett and Watson's (2002b) edited collection contains examinations of the home, romance and love, the street, the economy and consumption, the pub, community and space. Likewise Silva and Bennett's (2004) edited collection contains a similarly diverse coverage of areas, and Inglis (2005) is also in such a vein. While some of these of these areas will be considered in this book, I will focus on how the media connect with processes of place and space, family and sociation, work and enthusiasm. As will be seen, these derive from some of my own work as well as the emphases of much of the literature (see, for example, Moores 2000; Morley 2000).

Ordinary life

A key source for discussions of ordinary life is Raymond Williams' (1989) classic essay 'Culture is ordinary' (originally published in 1958). In this essay, Williams in many ways initially codifies what were to become some key emphases of cultural and media studies. He rejects two other ways of thinking of culture and its development. First, he argues that cultural elitism should be opposed. Williams' idea of culture is not confined to the processes of 'high' culture and he rejects cultural snobbery. Second, he expresses his opposition to the increased commercialization of culture and especially to the operations of advertising and the way in which it is coming to dominate ever more processes of culture. Williams, therefore, seeks to formulate a theory of and research into processes of culture that are not simply those of the great works of literature, art, and so on or the commercialization of culture. While he does think that both of these areas can be studied and critiqued (and he spent much of his work in so doing), they need to be rethought in different contexts.

Williams develops his critique and argument in the name of two main ideas and emphases. First, he argues that culture should be seen as a way of life (in an anthropological sense) with a strong historical background. As part of this emphasis on the way of life, Williams also argues for the significance of cultural creativity. It is strongly his view that culture changes over time and that moreover, people have the power to effect its change through their everyday actions. Second, culture as a way of life is social in that it is created, learned and lived in common with other people. In this sense Williams emphasizes the idea of a common culture. Moreover, in addition to being social, culture is also individual in that it is concerned with experience, personal effort and meaning.

These are arguments that have been influential and which can be followed in their significant emphases. In is important to recognize the dynamism of culture as inherited, learned, changing and changed through modes of human action. Second, that culture is social in that it is produced through human interaction, but also is woven into social conflict, social and cultural divisions and the constitution and reconstitution of communities. In these emphases, culture is political at a number of different levels. Third, culture is personal in that it is to do with individual identities and biography. In a term that Williams was very fond of, culture is *lived*. These three ideas that Williams emphasizes as key aspects of culture as a way of life are ones that I also seek to foreground as part of a theory and account of ordinary life: dynamism, social and personal.

While Williams provides a significant underpinning for a theory of ordinary life, his argument in this paper requires revision in two crucial ways. First, his emphasis on a common culture as a way of life, or often in his work as 'a whole way of life', cannot grasp the diversity and fluidity of cultures of ordinariness in a society such as that in the UK. It is essential that this trope of Williams is reconstituted to recognize the significance of ways of life, diversity and commonality and how ways of being in common and diversity are produced in the contexts of the flows of ordinary life. Something of this shift was captured by Grossberg (1996: 105) when he addressed the importance of the idea of community as defining 'an abode marking people's ways of belonging within the structured mobilities of everyday life'.

A second revision of Williams is to further emphasize, even more than he did, the *dynamism* of culture. Such a dynamism can, I suggest, be thought through how the processes of ordinary life and the ways in which they become of extraordinary significance to people in particular contexts of ordinary life lead to everyday cultural creativity and the investment of great value by people in processes and objects that have particular meanings for them. So in addition to ordinary life being dynamic, social and personal it is also about the interaction of the processes of ways of life and involves differential levels of investment by people that can be theorized in the interaction between the ordinary and the extraordinary.

In my account, ordinary life is both mundane and involves low and high investments in different types of process. This idea develops another emphasis in the work of Grossberg (1992), who has drawn a distinction between daily life and everyday life. For Grossberg, everyday life (which I will call ordinary life) has a number of luxuries, which are not available to those whose choices are limited by, for example, poverty and social exclusion (for whom Grossberg coins the term daily life). Thus, concerning everyday life, for him:

> There is a real pleasure and comfort in its mundanity, in the stability of its repetitiveness. Not only its practices but also its investments are routinized. In a sense, one need never worry about living within the maps of everyday life. Instead, one gets to 'choose' how one instantiates the maps, what matters, where one invests. In everyday life, one has the luxury of investing in the mundane and trivial, in the consumption of life itself. To offer the simplest example, there is a real security and pleasure in knowing when and where and exactly for what (including brands) one will go shopping next.
>
> (Grossberg 1992: 149)

Ordinary life provides a number of modes of security and routine (see also Silverstone 1994) that enable it to carry on. More recent work has also sought to develop some of these ideas from Williams and also to place increased emphasis on ideas of ordinary culture. In the context of the former, I will draw on the specific arguments of Couldry (2000a), which have also influenced other aspects of my thinking in this book. For the latter, I will begin the consideration through the work of Gronow and Warde (2001a and 2001b).

In *Inside Culture* (Couldry 2000a) offers a variety of important arguments concerning cultural studies and its future directions. While these are significant, I focus on a number of the points that he makes that are of particular concern for the argument and approach under development here. Couldry points out the significance of Williams' arguments concerning common culture, emphasizing that Williams was not simply replacing an elitist approach to culture with an anthropological one (p. 23). For Couldry, 'it is the complex interrelation of the "textual" and the "anthropological" approaches to culture which is important to his thesis' (p. 24). In an emphasis already briefly introduced, he argues in a way that makes the significance of the points exceptionally clear, that:

The concept of 'the ordinariness of culture' is important: first, because it looks at cultural production in terms of the contributions and reflections of all members of a culture; and second, because it stresses the political implications of how culture is organized, its material basis. Culture, in this sense, matters to everyone; it concerns our shared life together.

(Couldry 2000a: 26)

Despite what he sees as its many strengths, Couldry argues that Williams' work has limitations. First, he suggests that Williams' work tends to have a 'local' focus and, second, that it has difficulties in taking into account the changing nature of British communities, especially as they were changed by 'significant levels of government-encouraged immigration' (p. 29). These were compounded by Williams' difficulties in dealing with gender issues.

In broad terms, the latter difficulties have been recognized and discussed at least since Williams' work gained widespread influence. The critique by E. P. Thompson (1961) was only the beginning of this significant line of criticism when he suggested that Williams' idea of a whole way of life should be replaced by that of a 'whole way of struggle'. The former criticism is less securely based. While Williams' work was, in many ways, based on his experience of Welsh border community and this gives it a particular rootedness, it is important to recognize that this was indeed 'border country', which was always in Williams' work seen as connected to forces and movements outside it by networks of communication. In this sense Williams recognized very early that local living was in carried out in the context of global networks of communication, travel and the movement of capital to the disadvantage of organized labour.[1] Thus, it can be suggested that Williams' work is more important on these topics than Couldry allows. This may in one sense be a relatively small point, but it does facilitate the recognition that in many ways contemporary emphases on flows of people and information have always been a part of cultural studies.

In addition to his arguments concerning the significance of Williams' ideas of ordinariness for the study of culture, a second aspect of Couldry's argument is of importance. This is his point that cultural studies requires a fuller understanding of the individual. As he suggests, 'cultural studies has provided relatively few insights into how individuals are formed, and how they act, "inside" cultures. Post-structuralist critiques of the subject have only served to confuse matters' (p. 45). For Couldry, this means a concern with a range of individual voices and a refocus on the experiences of groups and individuals that have been relatively neglected in cultural studies. Two emphases here are of particular concern to my argument. First, he argues that 'cultural studies' work on television and film . . . has rarely, if ever considered the engagements of people with high cultural and/or economic capital' (p. 59). In drawing on some of my own research through the course of this book, I hope to rectify this omission, which I agree is serious for the project of understanding different forms of ordinary culture. Second, he maintains that:

People's engagement with 'ordinary' material culture (everyday clothes, household goods, and so on) and their dreams of material prosperity have normally been downplayed in cultural studies compared to more exciting, more conventionally 'cultural' interests (music, films, books, the leading edge of fashion).

(Couldry 2000a: 53)

In broad outline, this is important, although I will also suggest that it is also the case that topics such as music and film can be studied in different ways in the context of a theory of ordinary life. It is significant that Couldry's main point here has also been made in other more sociological and anthropological contexts that have focused on the study of consumption.

A good example of this is in the work of Gronow and Warde (2001a: 3), who argue that:

> The theories of consumption inherited from the last decade of scholarly inquiry have particular emphases, on choice and freedom, taste and lifestyle, identity and differentiation, image and appearance, transgression and carnival. However, these considerations left out a good deal of the substantive field of consumption. Those actions which required little reflection, which communicate few social messages, which play no role in distinction, and which do not excite much passion or emotion, were typically ignored.

Gronow and Warde (2001b) in accord with this view edited a text that sought to address the way in which too much emphasis had been placed on:

- extraordinary rather than ordinary items
- conspicuous rather than inconspicuous consumption
- individual choice rather than contextual and collective restraint
- conscious rational decision-making rather than routine, conventional and repetitive conduct
- decisions to purchase rather than practical contexts of appropriation and use
- commodified rather than other types of exchange
- considerations of personal identity rather than collective identification (Gronow and Warde 2001a: 4).

To a very large extent I share the view of Gronow and Warde, however, as with the point made with respect to Couldry, there is a further dimension, which is that activities and forms that have previously been considered as extraordinary can be considered in ordinary ways. Thus, it is not that attention needs to be paid to 'ordinary items' such as 'petrol for the car, the electricity for the light and the water for use in the new bathroom suite' (Gronow and Warde 2001a: 4), but forms and practices concerned with music and fashion might be considered in new ways. Furthermore, while collective identification is important, it is not to substitute for the analysis of modes of individual personal experience as I have suggested earlier. Thus, in many respects I continue to argue for the interaction of the ordinary and the extraordinary and the collective and the individual. I will have more to say on this below, but it is made in a discussion of radio (Longhurst et al. 2001) and can show the complexities of the relationships between the individual and the social, the ordinary and the extraordinary. A good way of showing this is through the consideration of the role of music in everyday life, which also allows an introduction of an area that has tended to be relatively neglected in previous studies of everyday life (Bull and Back 2003; Erlmann 2004; Hesmondhalgh 2002).

Music, sound and ordinary life

The following quotation taken from research where respondents were able to comment freely on the meaning of music for them (Crafts et al. 1993: 109) captures something of the significance of music in everyday life:

> Q   What does music mean to you?
> A   Music is just part of life, like air. You live with it all the time, so it's tough to judge what it means to you. For some people, it's a deep emotional thing, for some people, it's casual. I turn on the radio and it's there in the morning; it's there when I drive; it's there when I go out.
> Q   If it isn't there, do you miss it?
> A   No.
> Q   So you're not really aware that it is there?
> A   It's like a companion, or a back-up noise. Just something in the background. A lot of people turn the radio on and they're not listening to it for the most part, but it's there to keep them company, it's background noise. It's like the TV; they leave the TV on all the time, although it never gets watched. But it's background, people use it just to feel comfortable with.

Sociological work has deepened the understanding of the place of sound and music theoretically and empirically. An excellent example of this is the work of Tia DeNora (2000). The DeNora approach is premised in interactionist sociology. She explores how music is a part of the constitution of the interactions between people and how it plays a role in the constitution of the identities of those people themselves. Who we are and how we engage with other people are processes that are brought about significantly by interaction. DeNora points out that aspects of research on youth subcultural groups explored how music was a part of such interaction processes, and in her view a strength of this approach was its 'focus not on what can be said about cultural forms, but on what the appropriation of cultural materials achieves *in action*, what culture "does" for its consumers within the contexts of their lives' (p. 6).

In seeking to strengthen theoretically the descriptive approach of Crafts et al., DeNora considers three aspects of music's place in everyday life: its place in the constitution of our senses of self, or identity; its role in the construction of the body and the physical self; and its place in 'ordering' social relationships.

With respect to the first, DeNora shows how music is involved in the construction of feelings, as well as preventing the onset of undesired moods and feelings. For DeNora:

> Music is not simply used to express some internal emotional state. Indeed, that music is part of the reflexive constitution of that state; it is a

resource for the identification work of 'knowing how one feels' – a building material of 'subjectivity'.

(p. 37)

DeNora discusses a number of examples of this process and argues that:

> In none of these examples, however, does music simply *act upon* individuals, like a stimulus. Rather, music's 'effects' come from the ways in which individuals orient to it, how they interpret it and how they place it within their personal musical maps, within the semiotic web of music and extra-musical associations.
>
> (DeNora 2000: 61)

DeNora also shows in some detail how music is central to the constitution of the body and the physical self. A good example is her empirical study of the importance of music in an aerobics class. Thus, music 'defines the components of a session through its tempo changes (for example, music for warm up, core and cool down) and it also profiles the bodily movements associated with each of these components' (p. 92). Moreover, music is also involved in structuring how the body is deployed during specific aerobic movements. Music is far more than a background for those movements; it is core to how those movements are defined. As DeNora puts it: 'Following aerobics' musical changes and the ways in which real bodies interact with prescribed musical bodily changes, bodily changes allow us to examine the body, moment by moment, as it interacts with, and is configured in relation to, music' (p. 93). The aerobic body is (partly) constituted through the interaction with music, which is just a specific example of how 'music is, or rather can serve as, a constitutive property of bodily being' (p. 99).

Third, DeNora examines the way in which music is involved in the production and reproduction of ordered social life. Such social order is produced through a process of 'ordering'. Thus music can be implicated in the breakdown and reconstitution of social relationships. As DeNora comments on an interview with a woman who discussed music in the context of the breakdown of her marriage:

> Lesley describes how she began to make a deliberate musical move away from her relationship, replacing the 'popular jiggly' music that she perceived as within the bounds of the relationship – for example, Dire Straits – and also the more, as she perceived it, 'intellectual' mode of Radio 4, with music that her husband disliked and viewed with disapproval. Lesley goes on to describe how, near the end of the relationship with her ex-husband, she would sometimes, when she was angry play a Soft Cell song entitled, 'Say hello wave goodbye' (from an album called *Erotic Cabaret*).
>
> (DeNora 2000: 126–7)

The way in which television figures in such processes of relationship breakdown and family reconstitution is also shown clearly in the work of Gauntlett and Hill (1999). Music is also used in the ordering of the 'ordinary' consumption practices involved in shopping (DeNora and Belcher 2000).

Another important study that shows the role of music in everyday life in a different way was written by Bull (2000), who in general argues that 'there is no contemporary account of the auditory nature of everyday experience in urban and cultural studies' (p. 2). Bull deploys a detailed consideration of the role of personal stereos in the everyday lives of listeners, with a conceptualization of everyday life that draws on aspects of the work of Lefebvre and the Frankfurt School. His argument and research cover a wide range of issues. Most importantly, his detailed research on the way in which respondents use personal stereos is then used as a basis for the re-theorization of everyday life to take full account of the auditory dimensions.

Bull explores a number of aspects of personal stereo use (for a summary, see Bull 2000: 186–90) and the most significant are introduced here to illuminate the general trend of my argument. First, Bull discusses at some length how music users construct narratives – 'they enjoy playing a tape that reminds them of something in their own narrative' (p. 188) – to give pleasure to dull routines and how the personal stereo is used to manage the anxieties of urban living. He says the users' lifeworld 'is a lifeworld filled with potential anxiety concerning the threat of decentredness within a world of contingency in which the technologizing of experience becomes a successful antidote' (p. 43). 'Users often describe putting their personal stereos on as soon as they leave home with the purpose of "clearing a space" for themselves' (p. 189). For some female users personal stereos are used to create a space where they feel that they will not be so bothered by others – 'Personal stereos are visual "do not disturb" signs' (p. 189). Second, he carefully considers the complexities of the ways in which personal stereos enable the 'escape' from that which surrounds users, and how they go into 'dream worlds', which Bull sees as like films that the users construct drawing on bodily and visual experiences. In one sense, the personal stereo provides a soundtrack to the filmic transformation of everyday life on the part of the user. This is part of an argument that Bulls deploys concerning the interaction of aestheticization and technological change. Thus the technology of the personal stereo enables aestheticization that 'creates the world as an imaginary space, a projection of the desire of the user formulated within the cultural remit of the stock of their imagination which is mediated through the attendant sounds listened to' (p. 188). In an argument that has resonances for some of my own earlier (Abercrombie and Longhurst 1998) arguments and which will be further developed later in this book (see Chapter 4), Bull argues that 'personal-stereo users do not project themselves onto the world but rather construct the world narcissistically as projection of their own "mediated" sound world' (p. 188).

A key strength of the ethnographic work that Bull deploys and his interpretation of the results is that it shows how aspects of the mundane and the individual constitution of imagined spaces work in ordinary life. The mundane nature of that ordinary life is well captured in the following:

> City life is often experienced as repetitive and users are often consumed with their oppressive routine. They describe taking the same journey to work every weekday, forty-eight weeks of the year. They might also be fed up and bored with their job, their routine and their journey. They

know every step of the daily journey with its predictable monotony, every station and how long it will take them to cover their daily journey. They feel oppressed by it. They have long ceased to take any notice of their surroundings. The use of a personal stereo is the only thing that makes the time pass bearably for these users. At least whilst they listen to it they do not have to think about their daily routine or the office that awaits them. Personal stereos permit users to reclaim or repossess time.

(Bull 2000: 190)

In addition to therefore showing the ordinary and the repetitive, Bull also demonstrates how users move out of this routine (as well as the ordinary dangers and anxieties of the city) into the imagined and personally constructed pleasures of alternative realities. Bull uses these insights to argue that music and sound should be seen as a more important part of everyday life than has often been the case in the past, where there has been a significant visual emphasis to the detriment of the other senses. Despite its many insights and its significance to the sort of argument being deployed here, there are some deficiencies in this work. While the personal stereo users that Bull studied are described as commuting, sleeping and working and some of them have friends to share their stereos with, they often seem to be separated from wider networks of family and friends and other experiences. In some ways, these personal stereo users are rather like the separated (massified) individuals of mass culture and mass society theory. To develop this account further it is necessary to combine the sort of sophistication deployed by Bull with a similar degree of attention to the way in which family and friendship networks are culturally significant.

In addition, Bull downplays ideas of distinction. He does not discuss the work of Bourdieu and the sort of work produced on consumption by those influenced by Bourdieu. In one respect this may mean attention to the role of technological objects in status displays. In the area that Bull explores the function of the iPod in this respect is interesting, as it is most often seen simply as a fairly nondescript set of white earphones, even though this may be seen as an indicator of the status of the wearer as technologically advanced and a music lover with an extensive library of music as a resource. The possession of the iPod says something about the owner, but further allows a far greater range of sources for the materials that can be carried around to facilitate the modes of narcissism, narrative construction and aestheticization of everyday life described by Bull with respect to the personal stereo users. Thus while the routines described by Bull may have stayed much the same as travel to work has not changed much in recent years – except perhaps to be subject to even more pressures and greater dullness – the technologically facilitated means to manage it imaginatively have. Access to such goods and imaginative resources is, of course, dependent on other things such as money and a computer. However, in general as Nick Abercrombie and I argued in 1998, the media resources available in general are and continue to increase in ways that will change aspects of ordinary life.

Conclusion

I have argued in this chapter for a theory and account of ordinary life that combines a stress on the mundane and the routine with the study of the extraordinary pleasures that people find in their ordinary lives. Such an account sees social interaction with friends and family as critically important in a world that is increasingly media drenched. Moreover, it allows attention to the formation and reformation of identities and to people's desires to see themselves as individuals. Thus, while the theory of ordinary life encapsulates the mundane, it is not defined by it. People enjoy their ordinary lives as well as hating parts of it (as Bull's study shows). It is this dynamic and others that are crucial. However, I do not frame this in terms of now redundant overarching ideas of resistance to and incorporation into sovereign power sources.

To exemplify aspects of this position consider the following extract from an interview with a middle-class woman about her media use (Longhurst et al. 2001: 138):

Q You haven't got a video recorder, have you got satellite or cable?
A I've got a small portable with video player in it, but that's predominantly for the OU.
Q What about your daughter?
A Yes, she sometimes watches the cartoons. *Mary Poppins*, that kind of thing.
Q What about radio?
A All the time.
Q What sort of things?
A I have it permanently tuned to Radio 4.
Q In the home?
A Yes.
Q In the car?
A I would do in the car, but it's [mumble].
Q So what sort of things do you listen to if it's on permanently?
A *Today* in the morning, again in the afternoon.
Q But at other times during the evening?
A Yes, if I'm washing up. I like the 6.30 slot usually a comedy or a play and Saturdays I like because . . . No it's on whenever I'm in the kitchen. When I get through the door the first thing I do is switch the radio on. That's my Dad, my Dad always listened to the radio, that's where I get it from. G's [daughter] the same, she listens rather than watching. Comedy programmes, *I'm Sorry I Haven't a Clue, Desert Island Discs*.

The respondent locates her media use in her busy life and her Open University course. At the time when she was in the process of a divorce, from a husband who came from a 'higher' class position, she expresses the way in which her daughter's taste for radio is like hers. Moreover, the taste for radio is for the classic middle-class station of Radio 4. I argue that this encapsulates a number of themes introduced so far and further developed in the progress of this book. The process of media audiencing is performed in ordinary life and in the process of the interview. This involves modes of belonging (to the family and to educated middle-class groups), distinguishing (from those who watch lots of TV and listen to stations other than Radio 4) and individualizing (in that while tastes connect to others, she is still in control). These themes are taken up further later.

In this chapter, therefore, I have taken some of the initial steps in the development of the overall argument of the book. I have maintained that ordinary life is important, but that it is often theorized inadequately in the context of theories that are of little contemporary use in understanding complex social changes and is itself changing. Moreover, ordinary life is media drenched and is increasingly constituted around mediatized processes, but is not the same as media life. I have tried to exemplify some key aspects of this through the consideration of the importance of sound and music in ordinary life. The next step in my argument is to consider in more depth the key contextualizing social and cultural processes that are reconstituting ordinary life.

Note

1 This theme is important in Williams' novels, *Border Country* (1960), *Second Generation* (1964) and *The Fight for Manod* (1979).

3 Changing ordinary life

In Chapter 1, the introduction to this book, I exemplified how media are impacting on ordinary life by discussing the change in the range and amount of media technologies available in a contemporary home as compared with one 40 years ago. This should not be taken as suggesting that the primary way in which change is occurring is technological. While technological development is highly significant, I follow those critiques of technological determinism that argue that all such changes need to be seen as social through and through. In this sense such technological changes are socially contextualized by a range of other changes. An important part of my argument in this book is that the ordinary life in the way that I have characterized it in Chapter 2 is subject to change from a variety of forces and processes. Indeed, my contention is that the theories and accounts of everyday life that I reviewed in that chapter are unable to accommodate the significance of these changes. In this chapter, therefore, I consider four processes that have been identified in recent social and cultural research as having such overarching significance. There is a tendency in the literature to focus on one or more of these to the relative exclusion of the others. These themes will then figure and be examined in more detail in the chapters that follow. The four processes are: globalizing/hybridizing, fragmenting, spectacularizing and performing, and enthusing. In this chapter, I introduce key themes and processes in each of these areas to set the ground for my subsequent discussion.

Globalizing and hybridizing

As with everyday life, there is a voluminous literature on globalization and I only desire to be succinct at this point. Following the definition of globalization as 'the rapidly developing and ever-densening network of interconnections and interdependences that characterize modern social life' (Tomlinson 1999: 2) and seeing hybridization as the processes by which new interconnections between social and cultural forms are being produced in such a context, in broad terms it is possible to examine globalizing and hybridizing processes in four areas of practice and struggle: economic, political, social and cultural.

First, there is argument that capitalism and the business and economic processes that define it are spreading to all parts of the world. Thus, newspapers and academic literature discuss how companies like McDonald's or Starbucks are appearing in parts of the world (such as China) where, until recently, they would not have been welcome. Moreover, a related aspect of this process is how the practices of capitalist practice and organization have become parts of activities such as schools, hospitals and universities that are now considered as business. There is a strong economic logic to globalization. Second, there is the argument that political processes are increasingly globalized. This is often examined in terms of the decline of the nation state in the face of the economic strength of the capitalist enterprises that are core to the economic processes. However, it can also be thought of in terms of the way in which political processes are increasingly connected at global levels and how supranational government organizations are having an impact. Third, there are range of social practices thought of in terms of social interaction that are becoming globalized. Thus, there is the way in which the movement of people is being affected by the increased availability of cheap airfares and the movement of migrant workers. The latter is having an impact on the nature of the major cities of the western world in many ways. Even if the places to which people in a society like Britain travel are routinized and are themselves globalized, there is still a measure of new forms of social interaction that are taking place. The same is true for culture as ways of life and artistic production and consumption. On the one hand; there are processes that suggest that ways of life are converging (again as partly driven by the processes considered so far). Thus, we can get a similar coffee in Starbucks or a burger in McDonald's or we can shop for books and CDs in stores that appear increasingly similar. On the other hand, however, as part of this process as with others, there are new forms of ways of life and symbolic representation that develop that combine forms of artistic expressions and ways of life to produce new hybrids.

Three major points about these processes require emphasis. First, they are dynamic and (in some ways potentially) contradictory – thus, globalization does not mean that everything is becoming the same. As Tomlinson suggests:

> From the instrumental point of view of capitalism, then, connectivity works towards increasing a *functional* proximity. It doesn't make all places the same, but creates globalized spaces and connecting corridors which ease the flow of capital (including its commodities and its personnel) by matching the time-space compression of connectivity with a degree of cultural 'compression'.
>
> (Tomlinson 1999: 7)

What is occurring is what Tomlinson (1999: 9), following Robertson, terms 'unicity' – 'a sense that the world is becoming, for the first time in history, a single social and cultural setting'. It is important, therefore, to recognize the dynamic nature of the process, rather than seeing it as a simple unfolding of some kind of evolution.

Second, the different aspects of globalization are connected. Thus, any aspect of globalization analytically separated will condense and contain aspects of the other processes. Thus, the consumption of a CD as part of a way of life of an individual will depend on the social interaction of those who made it, who may be globally separated, the political processes that facilitate trade and the economic patterns of production and organization that led to it being produced and marketed in the first place.

Third, the practices of globalization are contested and struggle takes place around them. This may be the overt struggle that has led to violent and explicit confrontations around specific meetings of the global elite, organization of pop/rock concerts, and so on. However, the practices of hybridization also involve modes of contestation as well as accommodation and the production of new forms through collaboration.

Good examples of these interactions around globalization and hybridization can be found in the processes of production and consumption of popular music. These illuminate the complex reconstitution of cultural forms rather than the flattening out or elimination of a local form by the juggernaut of globalized sameness. There are a number of examples of this dynamic process (Bennett 2000; Taylor 1997). Ho (2003) analyses the development in Hong Kong of Cantopop (music that is sung in Cantonese). He argues that this form developed in the 1970s as part of a desire for music sung in the local language rather than in English or Mandarin Chinese. This can be seen as a process of localization. However, as time passed, Cantopop has been developed by the globalized large companies of the music industry and has been influenced and hybridized by music from other parts of the world. Ho argues that through this process, Cantopop has become multicultural. Indeed, as pressure has developed to increase market share as a part of what can be seen as a globalizing process, Cantopop artists now sing in Mandarin as well as Cantonese and have explored a range of different genres, not just 'formulaic romantic ballads and brain-dead dance tunes' (Ho 2003: 151). In Ho's argument, Hong Kong pop has been influenced by music from the USA and Britain, as well as Japan, China, Taiwan and Korea. In the production of 'new creative fusions':

> The story of Hong Kong pop in its global-local interaction is not only a case of cultural (western) imperialism and the Asianisation of Asia, but also involves a process of negotiated cultural identities as expressed in the language of Cantonese and other representational means.
>
> (Ho 2003: 154)

A key theme in the debate about globalization and hybridization is that of *local belonging*. I will take this up in some detail in Chapter 5 and, as with other aspects of this debate, only seek to introduce it here. In the earlier period of consideration of globalization, it was often suggested that the significance and meaning of local culture and local ways of life were being overrun by the globalized processes. This sort of idea was in continuity with earlier ideas of cultural imperialism, and so on. Apart from the impact of globalized cultures, it has also been argued that mobility affected the commitment of people to local areas and their perception of those areas themselves. In a common phrase, 'roots' were being replaced or overrun by 'routes'. Such a dichotomous simplification has little purchase, even if it were ever meant to in such a simplified way. As Tomlinson (1999: 29) argues: '[W]e need to see "roots and routes" as always coexistent in culture, and both as subject to transformation in global modernity.' This is now a dominant position in the dynamic of globalization and hybridization, one that maintains that the are 'glocal' cultures and that 'globalization promotes much more physical mobility than ever before, but the key to its cultural impact is the transformation of localities themselves' (Tomlinson 1999: 29). This position has been argued most fully and in most detail with respect to the media by Morley (2000). Thus, it is possible to see the issue of the form and meaning of modes of local belonging as a critical issue in contemporary sociology. I will seek to examine this with respect to two themes. First, there is the role of media in the constitution and reconstitution of modes of belonging to localities and social networks. Second, and in a related way, there is the consideration of what is actually meant by belonging. This means examining the extent to which modes of local belonging relate to other modes of belonging and 'rootedness'.

Modernity, fragmentation and personal choice

Discussions of globalization are often tied up with those about modernity. Sociology has always been concerned about the nature of modernity and from the 1980s onwards social science and the humanities conducted a contentious and often confused debate about whether society and culture had become postmodern. This debate has now almost vanished (Matthewman and Hoey 2006). On one level, this is welcome, as the terms in which it was conducted were becoming less and less likely to aid further insight. On another level, this is problematic. This is because a number of the themes that were explored in the postmodern debate continue to be of significance. Some of these are captured by terms such as hybridization, as the postmodern debate was concerned to explore the ways in which forms of culture and texts influenced each other in complex ways and how new forms that combined previously separate forms of culture were coming into being. However, another important concern of discussion was the extent to and ways in which cultures and forms of culture were fragmenting. An aspect of this discussion was the decline of the so-called grand, master or metanarratives that no longer governed cultures. While this theme from Lyotard (1984) was itself subject to some dispute, it did draw attention to ideas of local, relative and fragmented forms of life. Moreover, the discussion itself drew significant attention to the ways in which culture can be seen as changing – often in rapid ways. In some respects the debate on postmodernism became entwined with that on consumerism.

Another reason to mourn the premature death of the postmodern debate is that much of the sociological form of it was conducted with little reference to empirical evidence. While for some this was logical in that some forms of postmodern reasoning would resist any such straightforward call to notions of evidence, for a sociological analytical account of the contemporary condition it was ultimately disabling. It is also paradoxical as since the death of the debate evidence has come forward that can facilitate some refinement of the terms of understanding. The postmodern debate therefore foregrounded some issues that I suggest remain of some significance to the understanding of society and culture. In this section, I explore further ideas of fragmentation and rapid cultural change, drawing especially on the work of Lipovetsky (2005). In addition I introduce research on the idea of the cultural omnivore (see also Chapter 8).

Lipovetsky's argument is that advanced western democracies have moved into a new phase of cultural and social life. The postmodern, which is not in this book discussed in any detail, has been overtaken by the hyper-modern.[1] For Lipovetsky, the postmodern was a transitional period between the modernity of the late nineteenth century to the mid-twentieth and the hypermodern that was born in the 1980s. The postmodern therefore enabled the birth of the hypermodern from the modern. The hypermodern continues the progress of three key areas or processes: 'the market, technocratic efficiency and the individual' (p. 32).

While he discusses all three, it is the consideration of what in his introduction to this book, Charles (2005) labels 'paradoxical individualism' that forms the core of Lipovetsky's argument, as it is the mode of individualism that captures the nature and dynamic of hypermodernity. Given that individualism can often be seen as fragmenting collective actions and modes of belonging, these themes are very important to the argument here. The form and content of this hyperindividualism are summarized by Lipovetsky in a further three themes, which he says describe a 'society of fashion': 'ephemerality, novelty and permanent seduction' (p. 36). Lipovetsky's discussion rests on his earlier work on fashion (Lipovetsky 1994). Here, Lipovetsky examines the meaning of fashion, its development and, most significantly, how the processes involved in the changing modes of fashion as dress have generalized to epitomize contemporary cultural and social life. The processes involved in fashion have become extended across many different aspects of life. Lipovetsky referred to this as 'consummate fashion' and saw it through the lens of the three similar processes of 'ephemerality, seduction, and marginal differentiation' (1994: 131).

As fashion has democratized and spread as a principle it has allowed the individual freedom to define who they are, to consume more and a greater variety of goods and services. This mode of individualism can be seen as a form of fragmentation into increasingly smaller lifestyle enclaves. For Lipovetsky, it also means that the individual has become more reflexive and thus able to choose outside tradition and constraint how they perform who they are and how, for example, they attach themselves to political movements. Lipovetsky ranges wide across regions of social life to show how these processes are working out in different fields.

The most innovative and useful part of Lipovetsky's analysis for my argument rests with his consideration of the paradoxes of hypermodernity and hyperindividualism. The current hyperindividualism of the hypermodern as characterized by fashion is double edged, 'we' are both disciplined and free and we constrain ourselves but assert our individualism. In further individualizing and fragmenting, society is not becoming simply atomized, with no connections between people. However, the nature of the connections between the fragments and the hyperindividuals are becoming more contingent and subject to ongoing change and relative lack of constraint. Social capital (see later), to adopt a term that Lipovetsky would not use, given his critiques of Bourdieu, is fluid in this sense. Both Charles (2005) and Sennett (1994) point to the implications of this argument for politics, in that it makes political attachment more contingent and also in Lipovetsky's argument makes democracy work as in a sense it is more like a marketplace of choices. This is not a disciplined or one-dimensional culture, individualism or politics.

A key part of the importance of this for this book is that it characterizes a paradoxical (hyper) modernity in a way that is reminiscent of earlier work on modernity (e.g. Berman 1983; Giddens 1990) examined the paradoxes of classical or earlier modernity. It captures important aspects of society and culture as dynamic. I will return to these themes, but for the moment I want to emphasize the point that what may be seen as forms of social and cultural fragmentation and individualism can through the lens of this argument have forms of paradoxical aspects. People can be connected through culture and practice but there is more choice about how those connections are made and remade. Thus, there is contingency, fragmentation and individualism but also modes of connection. Some different aspects of this process can also be seen through the idea of the omnivore thesis.

This idea has been developed by Richard Peterson with a number of co-authors. For example, Peterson and Kern (1996), argue that in the USA there has been a shift from a division between the elite and the mass in culture. In particular, they argue that the middle class has become more omnivorous in taste (Peterson and Kern 1996) in that middle-class people engage with a wider range of cultural forms than was the case in previous historical periods and that they tend to treat them as equal. So, for example, in the past, an educated middle-class person might consume the classics of literature and classical music, they are now likely to read detective novels, watch soap operas on TV and listen to popular music from around the world as well. They are thus omnivores in that they consume both high and popular culture. As Peterson and Simkus (1992: 169) argue:

> There is mounting evidence that high-status groups not only participate more than do others in high-activities but also tend to participate more often in most kinds of leisure activities. In effect, elite taste is no longer defined as an expressed appreciation of the high art forms (and a moral disdain or bemused tolerance for all other aesthetic expressions). Now it is being redefined as an appreciation of the aesthetics of every distinctive form along with an appreciation of the high arts. Because status is gained by knowing about and participating in (that is to say, by consuming) all forms, the term *omnivore* seems appropriate.

In accord with my theme in this section, this can be seen as a form of fragmentation of a previously coherent mode of middle-class culture. However, in accord with the argument derived from Lipovetsky it also means that new combinations of taste are produced. Further, according to this thesis, those at the bottom of the social scale are univore-like as their cultural consumption is more restricted and constrained by material factors (Bryson 1997). Evidence for the omnivore thesis was initially produced with respect to the consumption of music in the USA and has now been subject to empirical investigation and theoretical refinement in a number of other countries (see Peterson and Anand 2004). This has suggested that the patterns of omnivoric taste may vary according to the medium being considered. However, as will be further considered in Chapter 8, this does offer evidence on some of the issues introduced by the debate on postmodernism. I now introduce the key dimensions of the third key area of change.

Spectacularizing and performing

In an argument that will be more fully explored in the next chapter, Nick Abercrombie and I (1998) have argued that in the course of becoming more audience-like, contemporary societies have involved increasingly significant processes of spectacle and performance that are fuelled by different types of media processes. A good example of these processes can be seen in Crawford's (2004) consideration of the contemporary sports event. Locating his discussion in the context of consumption, Crawford argues that:

> The spectacle within the sport venue should not be viewed as a one-way process of production and consumption, in which the audience constitutes passive consumers of the spectacle – as the audience themselves often constitute an important role in the creation of the spectacle and atmosphere within the venue.
>
> (2004: 85)

Thus, as these processes have developed, the spectators at the event become very significant to the creation of the event as a spectacle and perform for the audiences at the event and for those who might be watching via, for example, TV. Thus, performers in the crowd will be shown on the screens that are in the venue itself – 'the advent of large screen televisions at many contemporary sport venues allows *key performances* to become *key spectacles*; as these are selected by the venue's cameras and displayed on the screens and scoreboards' (Crawford 2004: 86). In addition, these performances will also be shown as part of the event to the wider audiences that are watching the event in homes and bars. The dressing up (or indeed undressing, as for example, men attending football matches without shirts become selected for wider transmission) shows how spectacle, performances and audiencing are interlocked.

Crawford also shows how the presence of the cameras at such events can be seen as part of a process of social control and surveillance. The increased presence of speed cameras involves the same sort of dualism: they keep drivers under surveillance, but the driver has to perform certain acts for them. Discussions of the sorts of processes of surveillance that are involved here are very common. Their main theoretical warrant is usually derived ultimately from the classic work of Foucault (1979), sometimes combined with some Weberian themes on bureaucratic control. However, this is only half the story. The reason why this is so has been most elegantly argued by Mathiesen (1997).

Mathiesen summarizes how, through the opening to *Discipline and Punish* (1979), Foucault draws attention to three processes of change: first, from physical punishment to penal incarceration; second, from 'torture of the body to the transformation of the soul' (p. 216); and, third, the 'broad historical change of social order' (p. 217). Thus, in drawing on Bentham, for 'Foucault, panopticism represents a fundamental movement or transformation *from the situation where the many see the few to the situation where the few see the many*' (p. 217). This is often taken as the major historical trend that has led to panoptical surveillance systems characterized by CCTV and so on. Mathiesen's argument is that Foucault and the Foucauldian approach are at best half-correct. Mathiesen argues that actually parallel to the panopticon and panopticism is the synopticon, where the many see the few, and therefore a process of synopticism.

For Mathiesen, panopticism and synopticism are parallel processes that have three aspects. First, he argues that both of the processes have accelerated in 'modern times'. Thus, while panopticon-type surveillance has progressed, so have technological forms and practices that enable the many to see the few through media including the press, film, radio and TV. The media thus, in some ways enable audiences to see the processes of power (or at least representations of them) and to view the activities of powerful people. Second, while these processes have accelerated in modernity, they are both long-established modes of power. Mathiesen argues that, 'the models of both systems go back far beyond the 1700s, and that they have historical roots in central social and political institutions' (1997: 222). Third, that they 'developed in intimate relation, even fusion with each other' (p. 223), as exemplified by the way that the Catholic Church used surveillance as well as vast cathedrals. Thus, Mathiesen's argument is that we are both seen by power and see it. Both of these processes involve performance and audience processes.

Documentary filmmaking and recording can be seen as involving both of these processes in different ways. Thus, the project of Mass Observation as part of the study of everyday life discussed in the previous chapter, can involve a small number of people surveying the many, but can then be displayed for a larger audience. Such ideas can also be seen in the current phase of the development of documentary in what Corner (2002) has termed 'documentary as diversion' or 'popular factual entertainment'. Thus, currently very popular reality TV programmes often involve surveillance and entertainment, participation and performance. In Corner's view we are in a 'postdocumentary culture'. Thus, reality TV of this type offers a good example of the interlocking of performance, spectacle and modes of surveillance.

My argument is that these processes are fuelled by media and technological innovation and this will be more fully grounded in the next chapter, but at the current juncture I want to stress how these activities are sedimented into ordinary life through a range of processes, but also the complex relations to the way in which power is exercised in different ways and in different contexts. Thus, power involves the spectacle of display as well as the surveillance of populations in ways that are intertwined in the ways that Mathiesen explains. The final process that I introduce in this chapter is enthusing.

Enthusing

I consider the idea of enthusing, by which I mean the ways in which people invest parts of their ordinary culture with significant levels of meaning, in detail in Chapter 9. At this point, I introduce the two main sources of the discussion that I will pursue. These are, first, the debates on the idea of social capital and the idea that it is in decline in advanced western democratic societies. Second, there are the now many analyses of media-based fandom. These literatures have tended to follow rather different paths, but I will argue that they have useful light to throw on one another.

The basic idea of social capital is both deceptively simple and historically well known. It is that social connections are significant in binding societies and cultures together and that the stronger these ties are, the more likely it is that people will trust one another. In contemporary social science there are two important sources for the way in which I will discuss these ideas in the book. First, there is Bourdieu's work on capitals and, second, the thesis on the decline and changing forms of social capital that has been most significantly developed by Putnam.

Bourdieu has been particularly influential in the English-speaking world through his work on culture and distinction (Bourdieu 1984). Bourdieu was, as nearly all sociologists are, concerned with the relationship between structure and agency. One way in which he addressed this debate was through the idea of practice, which is captured in the idea of 'agents' engagement with the objective structures of the modern world, crystallized into those patterns of relations, with their specific determining force, that we call "fields" (economic power, politics, cultural production, etc.' (Fowler 2000: 1). Human beings internalize structures, and actively live them out within habitus. It is important to retain the emphasis on practice and activity that this involves. For Bennett and Silva (2004: 7), Bourdieu 'wished to stress the creative, active, and inventive capacity of social actors while avoiding any notion of a transcendental subject'. Moreover:

> The concept does not form a part of any generalised account of social stasis resulting from a singular structure of repetition characterising the everyday, Indeed, the intelligibility of such a contention is disputed as the everyday inevitably becomes pluralised in being dispersed across different habituses.
>
> (Bennett and Silva 2004: 7)

The habitus includes our habits and our dispositions to classify the world-specific ways that relate to our social positions. The habitus or habituses (following Bennett and Silva) are not simply mentalistic or concerned with knowledge, but also concern our bodily habits and physical modes of movement.

For Bourdieu, class is the critical determinant of the habitus in which we live, but it should also be theorized as conditioned by gender (e.g. Adkins and Skeggs 2004), ethnicity and region, and so on. As has been argued, there are clear links with Butler's idea of performativity (see Butler 1997: 127–63; Salih 2002: 113) and the emphasis on performance that I have introduced so far.

These ideas are further explored in the rest of this book and at present I simply want to emphasize how the habitus is not simply a given, but is produced through modes of social and cultural interaction. The idea of the habitus has already been influential in thinking through the ways in which our positions in the world are structured and lived and I will seek to further develop such arguments in what follows.

It has been important to introduce the way in which Bourdieu theorizes the habitus, to contextualize his theory of capitals in structure, agency and practice. Bourdieu has been critical in contemporary social science in developing the idea of capital and applying this idea in new ways. As Lin (2001) shows, this has been a significant general movement in the social sciences, which has elaborated some basic Marxist insights. As is well known, for Bourdieu, there exists the economic capital that derives from money, income, economic investments, and so on and also cultural, social and symbolic capital. In general, in this idea 'there is a class, capitalists that controls the means of production – the process of pedagogic action or the education institutions (in homes, in schools and so on. In addition, there is more attention to the more micro social processes of capital deployment' (Lin 2001: 16). Cultural capital is made up of phenomena and practices such as knowledge, ways of life, ways of understanding the world and prestige. There are three main forms of cultural capital: embodied in 'long-lasting dispositions of the mind and body', objectified 'in the form of cultural goods' and institutionalized 'resulting in such things as educational qualifications' (Skeggs 2001: 296). Social capital is based on social networks, connections or relationships. Symbolic capital is 'the form the different types of capital take once they are perceived and legitimated as legitimate. Legitimation is the key mechanism in the conversion to power' (Skeggs 2001: 296). Capitals can be converted from one form to another, could oppose each other or can be stored and therefore gain interest. For example, those with high economic capital (who are wealthy), can purchase a high-status education for their child, which could then provide them with forms of cultural capital in educational qualifications and understanding of 'high' culture such as literature and art. Attending high-status (and costly) schools may also provide a network of contacts (such as the often cited 'old boy network') that might continue at university and in future life.

Another crucial idea that Bourdieu developed is that of field. A field is a region of social life that has its own set of rules and expectations. Some forms of capital may be very important in some fields, but less important in others. However, it is possible to move between fields using the conversion of capitals. Thus, economic capital may be of prime importance in the economic field, but it can also be used to advantageous effect in the political field.

It is important therefore to recognize the contextual importance of Bourdieu's work to the idea of social capital, especially as this idea has been significantly developed by Putnam (e.g. 2000) in recent years. Putnam's basic idea is deceptively simple. He argues that social capital has declined in the USA, especially in the period since the Second World War and that while there are a number of social factors that have contributed to this decline; the most significant is the increased amount of time devoted to the viewing of television. It is important to recognize how Putnam defines social capital:

Whereas physical capital refers to physical objects and human capital refers to properties of individuals, social capital refers to connections among individuals – social networks and the norms of reciprocity and trustworthiness that arise from them. In that sense social capital is closely related to what some have called 'civic virtue.' The difference is that 'social capital' calls attention to the fact that civic virtue is most powerful when embedded in a dense network of reciprocal social relations. A society of many virtuous but isolated individuals is not necessarily rich in social capital.

(Putnam 2000: 19)

Thus three features of this definition – 'networks, norms and trust' – are the triad which dominates conceptual discussion' (Schuller et al. 2000: 9). While in Putnam's earlier work there was a clear trend to think of social capital as a positive thing, more recently he has recognized the potentially dark side of social capital. For example: 'Networks and the associated norms of reciprocity are generally good for those inside the network, but the external effects of social capital are by no means always positive' (Putnam 2000: 21). In some respects those things that bind some groups together, and thus build social capital, are forms of exclusion of other groups and can therefore be socially pernicious. Aspects of this are picked up by Putnam in his distinction between bridging and bonding social capital:

Of all the dimensions along which forms of social capital vary, perhaps the most important is the distinction between *bridging* (or inclusive) and *bonding* (or exclusive). Some forms of social capital are, by choice or necessity, inward looking and tend to reinforce exclusive identities and homogeneous groups. Examples of bonding social capital include ethnic fraternal organizations, church-based women's reading groups, and fashionable country clubs. Other networks are outward looking and encompass people across diverse social cleavages. Examples of bridging social capital include the civil rights movement, many youth service groups, and ecumenical religious organizations.

(Putnam 2000: 22)

In this respect the focus or the scale of the group to which attention is drawn matters in debates about social capital. While there is a significant debate on Putnam's work, which has explored a number of critical issues,[2] it has been significant in drawing attention to the role of networks, formal and informal association in ordinary life. While, as will be shown, this focus has been arrived at from other directions as well, Putnam is an important source. For my current purposes, two critical issues arise, from Putnam and indeed from Bourdieu. First, there is the relationship between social and cultural capital. Second, there is the need to more fully understand the role of the media.

One of the problems of works on capitals is that there is a relative lack of consideration of the interaction between social and cultural capital. Therefore, Putnam's work, while recognizing that there are different sources of the idea of social capital, tends to be drawn to a political science focus on the implications of the decline in social capital for trust and civic consciousness. This is all well and good, but this is then relatively divorced from understandings of culture and cultural capital as involving a way of life or habitus (although not from the idea of cultural capital as manifested in institutionalized educational qualifications). This means that theorists and analysts like Putnam then neglect the way in which ways of life are changing with respect to a range of media and culture-based experiences. In short, TV becomes a 'bad thing' because it takes up the time that we could/should be devoting to those forms of associational activity that build trust and social capital. However, as has been pointed out (Norris 2000), this is a much generalized and indeed uninformed understanding of how people relate to TV and how it fits into ordinary life. It has been argued that it matters what people watch on TV. So that watching the news and documentary programmes might be thought to have a different relation to a person's views than watching game shows. However, even this is a very limited progression beyond the Putnam position, as it does not take account of the ways in which TV audiencing processes have been researched for over a half a century. Moreover, it even more clearly does not relate the complexity of our media and cultural lives to the complexity of our social ones – precisely a key point of my argument. A danger of Putnam's argument is that it nostalgically wants a return to a society that did not have the range of mass media resources that characterize contemporary advanced western democracies.

Switching tack somewhat, there is another literature that does consider in some detail the nature of investments that people make culturally and socially with the media. This is the now extensive material on media fandom. As was argued in *Audiences* (Abercrombie and Longhurst 1998) and as will be reviewed and extended later, this literature is relatively divorced from more sociological approaches to the patterns of social life. This has now begun to shift appreciably, so for example both the works of Crawford (2004) and Laughey (2006) (see further Chapter 4) show the interconnections between culture and media (theorized with contemporary resources) and social life. This is also the case with the work of Sandvoss (2005), who adopts an understanding of fandom that crosses a range of experiences:

> Whether we find our object of fandom in Britney Spears, *Buffy the Vampire Slayer* or the Boston Red Sox, these are all read and negotiated as (mediated) texts by their fans. The way in which fans relate to such texts and the performances that follow from this relationship vary between different fan cultures, and indeed from fan to fan. Yet, they are all forms of consumption in which we build and maintain an affective relationship with mediated texts and thus share fundamental psychological, social and cultural premises and consequences.
>
> (Sandvoss 2005: 8–9)

This idea of 'fandom as a form of sustained, affective consumption' (Sandvoss 2005: 9) captures significant aspects of contemporary social and cultural experience. Thus, it can be argued that these understandings of fandom need to be brought into closer conversation with new forms of understanding of the networked nature of social life. As I will suggest in the next chapter, Sandvoss' argument takes us a good way along that road, but more needs to be done to secure the dialogue that is necessary.

Conclusion

In this chapter, I have undertaken the discussion of the second broad strand of my contextualizing work in this book. On the basis of the characterization and theorization of ordinary life in Chapter 2, I have argued that there are four broad areas of social and cultural change that are impacting on and flowing through social and cultural life that are changing the processes of ordinary life. While these have technological outcomes, they are, I want to argue, more basic than that. In many ways it is important to recognize that these are not new processes in themselves. Thus, capitalism has always involved a globalizing logic that brings different forms of culture and ways of life into new interactions. Moreover, cultural change has often been characterized as involving fragmentation of previous organic cultures. In addition, as Mathiesen argues, the surveillance and performing processes of panopticism and synopticism are long-run historical processes. Likewise social and cultural capitals (as well as habituses and fields) are subject to processes of logic and change.

Despite this continuity, I argue first that these different processes have not been sufficiently examined in the ways in which their interrelations are impacting on contemporary ordinary life. Moreover, I argue that there is a need to understand their specific interrelations in the society and cultural form that has been captured in Lipovetsky's characterization of hypermodernity. Again as will be further discussed in subsequent chapters, thus it is possible to begin from his position that:

> Hypermodernity has not replaced faith in progress by despair and nihilism, but by an unstable, fluctuating confidence that varies with events and circumstances. As the motor driving the dynamic of investments and consumption, optimism in the future has shrunk: but it is not dead. Like everything else, the sense of confidence has broken away from institutions and become deregulated; it now manifests itself only as a series of ups and downs.
>
> (Lipovetsky 2005: 45)

These ups and downs can, in one sense, as I will further suggest, manifest themselves in the dynamic of the ordinary and the extraordinary. Having made these points, I now wish to bring together the strands so far to argue on the basis of some earlier work that this ordinary life should be seen critically as an audienced process based on spectacle, performance and audience processes.

Notes

1 There are, of course, a number of writers who have also used the term hypermodern. I think that the discussion by Lipovetsky has some important features that I draw out here.
2 This is now an exceptionally wide debate, but a good statement of many of the issues remains Portes (1998).

4 Understanding *and* theorizing cultural change

So far I have argued a number of general points maintaining that in the context of wide-ranging processes of social and cultural change it is crucial to develop a revised theory of ordinary life. This theory combines a focus on the mundane day-to-day events and practices that make up ordinary life, with increased attention to the ways in which media are structuring and restructuring a number of aspects of our lives. Morover, in the previous chapter I have identified, on the basis of recent literature, some key processes of socio-cultural change that provide an integrated context for this conceptualization of ordinary life. At several points, I have argued somewhat briefly that it is important that this ordinary life is seen as involving audience and performance processes. However, I have not fully grounded or contextualized that argument. That is the task of this chapter. This discussion will provide the third aspect of the background for the subsequent discussion in the book. I proceed as follows. I begin by considering issues of spectacle, performance and performativity outlining the significance of the spectacle/performance paradigm for the study of media audiences. This grounds my contention that these processes are at the heart of ordinary life. This leads to examination of important differences between audience positions and some critical research questions. It is important to emphasize that, once more, I will be selective.

Spectacle, performance and performativity

While increased research attention to media audiences has been important, future understandings will be limited unless reformulated in the context of audience change (Abercrombie and Longhurst 1998). Moreover, such changes require new modes of conceptualization. The two most important ways of conceptualizing the audience – the behavioural paradigm and the incorporation/resistance paradigm are limited in critical ways. The behavioural paradigm tends to consider the audience as individuals as either affected by the media (often in a pernicious way by, for example, propaganda or by particular representations of scxual activity, violcncc, and so on) or as individuals who use the media to fulfil certain wants and needs (in the so-called uses and gratifications approach).

There are a number of problems with this paradigm, including its restricted understanding of social life, its inattention to power relations and its lack of attention to the textual nature of media products. The behavioural paradigm was extensively criticized by the 'critical' approach to audience study (Hall 1980), or what can be termed the incorporation/resistance paradigm.

The incorporation/resistance paradigm, based on a sophisticated Marxist theory of capitalist and class exploitation, took power in society as crucial. The unequal structuring of society, especially in the earlier work done within its parameters in terms of class, but subsequently with respect to gender, race and age, was at the heart of the analysis. Its key research problem (with respect to audiences) concerned the extent to which and ways in which such social structuring and social location influenced the decoding of media texts. Media form and content have thus been reconsidered as text, rather than media messages or stimuli, in ideological terms. A critical research issue in this paradigm therefore is the extent to which audiences incorporated by dominant ideologies in media texts or to what degree they are able to resist them.

Influential studies carried out in this context examined the forms of incorporation to, negotiation with and opposition to dominant or preferred meanings in the main in ideological terms (Morley 1980). However, while a number of problems with this approach were recognized rapidly (Morley 1981) such as the tendency to overemphasize the coherence of the response to different texts, often in accord with one of the social bases, such as class or gender, or to conflate an active response to media with a critical one, the paradigm was hugely influential in audience research in the 1980s and 1990s. It had set the context for 'normal science' and 'puzzle solving'. The problem is that the findings from this normal science (as well as social and cultural changes) destabilized the paradigm. Empirical studies should have led to a potential questioning of their initial premises as interpretation was becoming increasingly strained. In this context, these empirical findings and changed audience processes can better be understood in the context of a new paradigm for audience research.

The argument for the spectacle/performance paradigm (SPP) rests on ideas that both audiences and conceptualizations of the audience were changing. It can be argued that there are three different and coexisting types of audience: simple, mass and diffused. The simple audience as exemplified by that at a theatre or at a sports event involves: relatively direct communication from performers to audience; a performance that takes place in a confined locale; and high ceremony as it is a special event, within a ritualized setting that is highly meaningful for participants. The performance and the audience response are public events and performers are separated from the audience by physical or social boundaries. The attention level of the audience with respect to the performance is high.

Mass audiences come with increasingly mediated communication. The best example of a mass audience is for television, although popular music and film also have mass audiences. Communication is highly mediated as the performance takes place a long way from the audience spatially and is now usually recorded at an earlier time and place. The text is edited for transmission. Through these processes, the relatively direct communication between 'live' performers and audience is broken. The texts of the television, music and film industries (which are subject to processes of technological convergence) are globally available (see the discussion of globalization in Chapter 3) and therefore are not discreet performances located in a time, place or space. Ritual and ceremony decline as texts and media become part of ordinary life. Thus, while some television viewing is highly ceremonial and 'meaningful', for example a group or a family may view a particular pro-gramme at a certain time, a number of studies have shown much TV viewing is distracted or done while other things are going on. The mass audience is private rather than public in the main. Even films are now commonly watched on video or DVD in the home. Television viewing, once the medium is established in a society, predominantly takes place in the home. Significant performative occasions such as watching a sports event in a bar are exceptions that prove the rule of the domesticity of the medium and the audience. The attention of the audience can vary from highly engaged, focused viewing to complete distraction. Finally, the distance in spatial and time dimensions of the audience from the performance is high.

The diffused audience is characterized as follows:

> The essential feature of this audience-experience is that, in contempor-ary society; everyone becomes an audience all the time. Being a member of an audience is no longer an exceptional event, nor even an everyday event. Rather it is constitutive of everyday life. This is not a claim that simple audiences or mass audiences no longer exist, quite the contrary. These experiences are as common as ever, but they take place against the background of the diffused audience.
>
> (Abercrombie and Longhurst 1998: 68–9)

Several social processes, which have been considered so far in this book, contextualize the development of the diffused audience. First, people are devoting increasing amounts of time to media consumption. Second, such consumption is increasingly woven into the fabric of ordinary life. Third, western capitalist societies have become more performative in a number of ways. Thus, many aspects of ordinary life have been subject to increased con-sumption activities that involve display and the performance of a spectacle. One example of this is the extension of performance and consumption around contemporary weddings (Boden 2003), which can now cost significant sums and which are fuelled by representation of celebrity weddings and magazines that offer advice on how the wedding is to be performed. 'Special' days during the year are also becoming increasingly consumer oriented in ways that prompt expenditure, as well as explicit performance and display. In Britain, this sort of spectacle–performance–consumption cycle, would include the fol-lowing: Christmas, New Year, St Valentine's Day, Mothers' Day, Father's Day, Halloween and Guy Fawkes Night. This cycle is punctuated by other regular events like birthdays and weddings, as discussed by Boden (2003), as well as occasions such as child-naming ceremonies. While this mode of performance is specific to contemporary and highly mediated societies, it is based on that from everyday life in earlier periods.

This sort of argument can be considered in the light of the influence of the work of Judith Butler, which has raised a number of fundamental issues about performance and performativity. It is worth exploring aspects of this approach to consider some potential ways in which further attention to performance and performativity can advance understanding of audiences in the context of the SPP and ordinary life. Given this aim, my discussion of Butler will inevitably be selective.

The crucial dimensions of Butler's approach are clear and now well known. As Bell (1999a: 3) says, 'gender to cut a long story short, is an effect performatively produced' and 'identity is the effect of performance and not vice versa'. Identities such as gender are therefore produced by practice (Butler 1999: 184) and the performance of them in social and linguistic processes, rather than being something pre-existing that is given expression in action and practice: As Butler argues, 'If gender attributes, however, are not expressive but performative, then these attributes effectively constitute the identity they are said to express or reveal' (1999: 180).

Salih (2002: 63) argues, that this sort of approach, which she represents through the following quotation from *Gender Trouble*: 'There is no gender identity behind the expressions of gender; that identity is performatively constituted by the very expressions that are said to be its results' (p. 25), has confused many people. How can there be a performance without a performer, an act without an actor? Actually Butler is not claiming that gender is a performance, and she distinguishes between performance and performativity (although at times in *Gender Trouble* the two terms seem to slide into one another).

Such potential confusion was recognized by Butler herself, and she has sought to address the issue in subsequent work. As she says in the 1999 Preface to *Gender Trouble*:

> Much of my work in recent years has been devoted to clarifying and revising the theory of performativity that is outlined in *Gender Trouble*. It is difficult to say precisely what performativity is not only because my own views on what 'performativity' might mean have changed over time, most often in response to excellent criticisms, but because so many others have taken it up and given their own formulations . . . In the first instance, then, the performativity of gender revolves around this metalepsis, the way in which the anticipation of a gendered essence produces that which it posits as outside itself. Second, performativity is not a singular act, but a repetition and a ritual, which achieves its effects through its naturalization in the context of a body, understood, in part, as a culturally sustained temporal duration.
>
> (Butler 1999: xiv–xv)

To summarize, performance can be said to involve intention and action on the part of a constituted and volitional subject, whereas performativity is the processes that constitute the subject (and the body of the subject – Butler 1993). Butler argues 'that gender identity is a sequence of acts (an idea that has existential underpinnings), but she also argues that there is no pre-existing performer who does those acts, no doer behind the deed. Here she draws a distinction between *performance* (which presupposes the existence of a subject) and *performativity* (which does not). This does not mean that there is no subject, but that the subject is not exactly where we would expect to find it – i.e. 'behind' or 'before' its deeds – so that 'reading *Gender Trouble* will call for new and radical ways of looking at (or perhaps looking *for*) gender identity' (Salih 2002: 45).

There seem to be a number of strengths and potential ways forward from Butler, for a reconstituted theory of ordinary life as media drenched. Thus, Butler's approach points to the role of the enactment and re-enactment of identities in social life – 'Space does not disappear but is reconstituted: gone is metaphorical space – the continents of subjectivity habitable only by authentic substantive identities – and in its place is social space: the symbolic realm in which subjects interpellate and hail other subjects, in which performative enactment of gender occurs' (Lloyd 1999: 196–7).

This is very suggestive, as it allows for both some measure of agency and the recursive nature of social life (see the many works of Giddens that deploy this idea). As Butler recognizes and as has been explored by others, there are some significant parallels with Bourdieu here (see also Chapter 3). In this respect, it can be suggested that there is, at this point, some potential. However, for the purposes of this book, two key issues remain. First, there is the continuing confusion in the relationship between performance and performativity. Second, and even more pertinent, is the relative neglect of the audience in these theorizations. I wish to return to the former after discussion of the latter.

One of the striking things about much of the commentary on Butler's work is that it discusses the way in which there can be a performance without an acting subject, but that in relative terms it neglects the significance of the audience to the performance. It is significant that Butler herself seems to recognize the status of some of the issues involved. Thus, in the 1999 Preface to *Gender Trouble* she argues the following:

> Moreover, my theory sometimes waffles between understanding performativity as linguistic and casting it as theatrical. I have come to think that the two are invariably related, chiasmically so, and that a reconsideration of the speech act as an instance of power invariably draws attention to both its theatrical and linguistic dimensions. In *Excitable Speech*, I sought to show that the speech act is at once performed (and thus theatrical, presented to an *audience*, subject to interpretation) and linguistic, inducing a set of effects through its implied relation to linguistic conventions.
>
> (Butler 1999: xxv, my emphasis)

This is significant, although the place of the audience still requires theorization. A clear instance of some of the issues involved can be found in the following comment from an interview conducted with Butler in 1997:

> I do think that there is a performativity to the gaze that is not simply the transposition of a textual model onto a visual one; that when we see Rodney King, when we see that video we are also reading and we also

constituting, and that the reading is a certain conjuring and a certain construction. How do we describe that? It seems to me that that is a modality of performativity, that it is racialization, that the kind of visual reading practice that goes into the viewing of the video is part of what I would mean by racialization, and part of what I would understand as the performativity of what it is 'to race something' or to be 'raced' by it. So I suppose that I'm interested in the modalities of performativity that take it out of its purely textualist context.

(Bell 1999b: 169)

This is suggestive, but raises a number of questions for the scholar of audience processes and ordinary life: what/who is the we? What is the relationship between constituting, conjuring and construction? Are all raced in the same way? Are all the performative modalities of racing equal? Some of these questions are similar to those that arose out of some of the attempts to deal with some of the similar sort of literature that has informed Butler's work (for example Althusser and Foucault) within the incorporation/resistance paradigm in audience studies. Thus, in one respect Butler's comment suggests a version of incorporation and hegemony – an active constitution of the raced subject through interpellation that ultimately constructs a dominant racial order. In another respect there is the idea of the 'active' reader – the conjurer sounds not dissimilar to the poachers of the fan literature (e.g. Jenkins 1992) and the attempt to theorize the resistive and active audience. As noted earlier, the research question for 'normal science' in the paradigm is the balance between them. On yet another plane, we are returned to questions of the differential way in which audiences might be raced. The danger with these formulations is that by bearing the marks of a textualist- and ideologically driven set of theories, performativity ends by textually reinstating questions that *Audiences* sought to dispel (see also Butler 1997). Thus, Butler appears to end up on the ground of the extent to which audiences are incorporated or resistant. Or, to put it another way, in a social space defined by voluntarism and determinism (see, in a related vein, the discussion in Lloyd 1999). If this is the case, can Butler add anything to the arguments of the SPP?

Some general comments are germane. First, I argue that Butler's arguments cannot be accepted wholeheartedly because of the lack of an adequate theory of the audience. Second, where there are gestures in this direction in her work, these are limited by the framework that informs the premises of her work, which means that she is constrained by IRP-type issues. However, third, she does offer an important emphasis on how identities, bodies and social practices are in process through their constitution through performed activities. I will suggest that the best way to theorize this issue is through the idea of performing human beings.

Moving to another aspect of the SPP, Crawford (2004) adds to the understanding of the simple audience when he questions 'if audiences were ever *simple?*' and such arguments fall into a trap of 'presuming that face-to-face communication is by its very nature direct' or 'unmediated'. As he says, this 'ignores that even direct communication is "mediated" through language, signs, symbols, culture and power relations. Admittedly, the advent of mass communication adds further levels of mediation and distance between the audience and performer. However, this is not a move from the unmediated to the mediated, but rather needs to be understood as adding *additional* levels of mediation between the audience and performer' (Crawford 2004: 25). While this point is germane and it can be accepted without destabilizing the overall model, there is an important point to be made here. Crawford's argument reinforces that about the role of mass media of communication in leading to new types of audience experience. Thus, the points about the increased significance of media in varied audience experiences stand, showing the differences of this argument from those that use transhistorical ideas of theatricality and performance.

The development of the diffused audience of ordinary life is specifically a result of two interconnected social processes. First, there is the increasing spectacularization of the social world. Second, there is the way that individuals are constituted as narcissistic. The diffused audience is different from simple or mass audiences. Thus, significantly, the social (and indeed sometimes physical distance) between performers and audience is increasingly eroded. Consequently, communication between performer (or producer) and the audience is 'fused' and the role of mediating institutions becomes much less important. Social distance tends to be eroded. Such diffused audiences are both local and global as the performances of ordinary life are enacted in ordinary settings and use a range of resources to fuel the imagination. Hence, as introduced in Chapter 3, global processes and resources can be lived out in local and specific environments. The extent of ceremony in diffused audience processes tends to be relatively low. This is because they are enacted in the context of the flow of ordinary life.

However, certain aspects of that everyday life become highly ceremonial and invested with great meaning to become 'extraordinary'. Thus, for example, there is the rapid development in Britain in recent years of roadside shrines at accident points and a tendency to promote certain key birthdays by banners on the outside of houses. Attention is also subject to a degree of variability, as aspects of ordinary life and audience members switch from intense involvement to relative indifference, or what Goffman (1963) theorized as 'civil inattention'.[1] Performance in the diffused audience is both public and private and the boundaries between historically separated spheres of social life have been blurred, as in the processes theorized by Lash (1990) as de-differentiation.

Some writers have criticized the idea of power that this entails. Key works in this respect are by Crawford (2004) and Couldry (2005). Crawford argues that this sort of 'consideration of power relations is largely restricted to a critique of its centrality to the incorporation/resistance paradigm. However, beyond a few passing remarks to the increasing fragmentation of social power, this is subsequently ignored in their theorization' (2004: 26). Couldry makes a similar point in developing an argument concerning the way in which this argument tends to deflate the power of media institutions, which is real and apparent in a number of ways. Crawford uses the work of Mathiesen (see Chapter 3) and others to consider the place of power and Couldry seeks to show how media institutions are culturally significant in Durkheimian ways. It should, therefore, be apparent that there are some significant issues here, although they actually reinforce the argument for the SPP rather than detract from it. Thus, the point is that some Foucauldian ways forward are potentially more significant for audience study than quasi-Marxist ones and this seems to have been accepted. Perhaps the problem is in working this through more. Thus, I have begun to think about this issue in previous chapters, but will also explore a number of dimensions in what follows. However, I will be arguing that we need to pay attention to micro-powers in a range of social situations and that we need to take apart what is meant by the media, to explore the powers of different media in particular social contexts.

Crawford (2004: 25) argues that: 'Many single audience groups may cross-cut all three audience types, even at the same instance, and furthermore that this occurrence may be increasing.' He suggests that contemporary sports events are good examples where simple, mass and diffused audiences combine. While this is indeed a good example of the use of the typology, it does not represent a fundamental criticism of the model, for two main reasons. First, the fact that there are different audience positions within a social situation is part of the overall argument for the SPP. As society and culture become more spectacular and performance oriented, it will be expected that many social and cultural situations develop in the same direction. Second, there is still an important sense in which the sports event has a simple audience at its core. The event would not be available for the other modes of audience experience if the simple audience was not present. This is shown by the lack of 'atmosphere' when for disciplinary reasons a sports event takes place without spectators. Thus, while audience experiences may increasingly be intertwining, the simple audience is at the core. The interaction between simple, mass and diffused audience processes is a crucial point for attention (see further Longhurst et al. 2007). Neither the behavioural paradigm nor the incorporation/resistance paradigm is able to explore these interactions. The emergent spectacle/performance paradigm can, as it can consider how the audience is socially constructed and reconstructed (rather than being determined or structured) through the interconnected processes of everyday spectacle and narcissism. Attention should focus on the way in which media interact to form as mediascape (Appadurai 1993), rather than media messages or texts per se. This relocates analysis of media texts in an alternative framework. Rather than considering the effects, functions or ideological operations of the media, we need to understand the interaction between ordinary life, audience processes and identity formation and reformation. This does not mean that concepts such as class are irrelevant to this paradigm, rather, in an opposite way, it suggests that the analysis of the construction and reconstruction of, for example, class identities requires rather more attention than it has hitherto attracted (see further, Savage et al. 2001 and Chapters 6, 7 and 8).

Audience positions

In elaborating the SPP, there are five possible positions that audience members can occupy. At one end of this audience continuum is the consumer, who interacts with the media in a relatively generalized and unfocused fashion. The next place along the continuum is that of the fan, who is particularly attached to certain programmes or stars within the context of relatively high media usage. The next place is occupied by the cultist, who builds on such attachments to focus media and audience activities around certain key programmes. It can be hypothesized that cultists will also tend to interact more directly with those who have similar tastes. Their media activities provided a particular focus for modes of social interaction. Enthusiasts tend to be more involved in actual production of artefacts connected to their fan and cultic activities. The now 'classic' studies of fandom such as those of *Star Trek* fandom, point to the writing of stories and the making of videos and paintings (see, for example, Bacon-Smith 1992; Jenkins 1992; Penley 1992). Two of the most significant and recent discussions of fan processes have shown the need for further sophisticated discussion of the individual, self and identity in this context (Hills 2002; Sandvoss 2005). Sandvoss, in particular, draws on consideration of narcissism as one starting point. Aspects of this important literature will be further considered in Chapter 9 and it is clear that this is an area where further research and recent literature have much to add. However, Sandvoss's general point is well made:

> For all the attention to the social and cultural context of fan consumption in the approaches to fandom discussed so far, the psychological basis of the pleasures, desires and motivations that form the relationship between given fans and their objects of fascination have remained comparatively unexplored and under-theorized.
>
> (Sandvoss 2005: 67)

Sandvoss explores three psychoanalytic approaches 'on the motivations and pleasures of fandom' (p. 94): Freudian, Kleinian and Winnicott's idea of the transitional object (which is also of significance in Silverstone's (1994) work). While all these approaches are used in Sandvoss's work there are problems with them that reveal the scope for an alternative account. He argues for a theory of self-reflection, 'as fans are fascinated by extensions of themselves, which they do not recognize as such' (p. 121).

> Self-reflections are manifested on a number of levels; in fans' failure to recognize boundaries between themselves and their object of fandom, in a range of identificatory fantasies of resemblance or imitation, and in the construction of readings of objects of fandom that move from a characterization of the fan text to the characterization of the fan him- or herself.
>
> (Sandvoss 2005: 121–2)

While, it may be argued, this suggests at least by implication a measure of pathology, which I am sure is not the intention, it does offer ways of thinking that once combined with other accounts can contribute to an account of how individuals are constituted and reconstituted in a media-drenched society. It should also be noted that this goes beyond the theorization of fans, as it can be argued that these processes have more general pertinence, as will be explored.

The final point on the continuum is that of the petty producer who is reaching the point where enthusiasm is becoming professionalized into a full-time activity (see Crawford 2004; Moorhouse 1991). The identification of this continuum allows further differentiation in contemporary audience positions than had hitherto been the case.

However, Hills (2002, 2005) argues that this portrays consumers in a negative way, especially in the context of an audience continuum:

> Abercrombie and Longhurst's model reproduces exactly the type of moral dualism which places 'good' fandom in opposition to the 'bad' consumer. They view 'the consumer' as somebody who has the least amount of skill that they define and study. This view of the consumer is an essentially negative one: consumers lack the developed forms of expertise and knowledge that fans, enthusiasts and cultists all possess in ever-increasing and ever-more-specialised forms.
>
> (Hills 2002: 29)

However, the warrant for this argument seems thin. While it is possible to discuss the range of particular skills that distinguish points along the continuum, I do not argue that a 'moral' judgement is involved. It would be just as plausible to say that the continuum morally judges the fan or cultist for his/her investments in activities that some would see as trivial. Actually neither of these positions is correct. I am not critical of consumption per se, rather, consumption is an aspect of ordinary life that is increasingly important, although I also think that while many of us are knowledgeable in consumer activities, we are more knowledgeable about other things that mean more to us. For example, the car for me is a consumer object; I like some and not others in the sense that the design appeals to me or not and it is a convenient technology (sometimes) to get me around, but I have little enthusiast investment in it – I don't like to tinker, don't like car racing, and so on. By contrast I am much more fan-like about popular music. On these terms, I make no moral judgement about those who possess skills with respect to cars or those who do not. Especially as those who possess such skills can often be of use to those of us who do not. Therefore, with respect to fandom, there is not a moral argument and we sought a useful characterization for further theoretical and empirical work. It is, of course, possible to consider political and resource issues about car fandom, but that seems to me to be a different register of discourse.

There are also other issues with the continuum. Thus, it can also be argued that the audience continuum, as well as being a useful typology 'may represent a possible career path under certain conditions' (Abercrombie and Longhurst 1998: 141). The key influence here is the work of Stebbins (1992), but Crawford has now developed the argument, in his discussion of the potential 'career progression of a sport fan' (Crawford 2004: 42–9). This introduces a number of additional aspects to the continuum that we identified and therefore takes the model forward in a number of important ways. However, the basic idea remains intact.

Research questions

The argument for the SPP rests on the claims about the social processes that were changing to produce the paradigm and that research studies were appearing that could be best understood and used from within this context. The argument sets a research agenda that has a number of components. First, in accord with the claims about ordinary life made above, it is important to begin research on the local level and to consider processes of belonging. This does not rule out considering the place of globalization (see Chapter 3) and global media, or mean the return of nostalgic concepts of face-to-face community (see further, Savage et al. 2005 and Chapter 5), but enables analysis of the interaction between the local and global in concrete places, where most people live (see also, for example, Morley 2000). Second, the significance of identity formation and reformation in ordinary life needs research across a range of dimensions. It is important to stress that one of the key research questions is the *relative* importance of the connection to particular media in this sense, rather than any assumption that any one medium is of most importance (for example, on the relative importance of radio, see Longhurst et al. 2001; and on the relative importance of popular music to young people, see Carrabine and Longhurst 1999). This rests on the argument that those who are studying a particular medium tend to overemphasize its importance across the social spectrum and to individuals.

A good example of a study that has taken the agenda of examining contemporary relative media use forward is that by Laughey (2006). He demonstrates how fluidity of commitment by young people to different forms of music is played out in personal terms as well as a range of public performances. This captures the way in which music flows through contemporary life in a range of interacting ways. Laughey's work is based on detailed research on young people in the north-west of England and I can only briefly comment on some of it.

Laughey argues against the ways in which music use has been situated within approaches that emphasize and deploy the idea of youth subculture. While there are now a number of conventional criticisms of this literature, which have been rehearsed in a number of places, Laughey takes a particular slant. For example, he shows how such theories have tended to emphasize generational conflict and separation rather than influence. Moreover, he argues that there are subtle shifts in musical taste within a generally wide-ranging set of tastes:

> Two types of narratives about music tastes and performances that accorded to different timeframes will thus be substantiated: narratives that are embedded – frequently in family contexts – through memories facilitated by (domestic) music experiences; and narratives that are radically contextualised (Ang 1996) – frequently in peer group contexts – in immediate relation to the whims of music fashions.
>
> (Laughey 2006: 5)

In accord with my argument for an understanding of ordinary life as based in audience interactions and performances, Laughey explores the complex dynamics between the personal tastes and the public performances of a range of musically based practices. An important part of this discussion is where he shows the different positions that are taken up by young people with respect to music. He discusses these positions along two particular dimensions:

first, the degree of involvement with music, which he divides into casual and intensive; and, second, whether the tastes and practices are inclusive or exclusive. Combining these dimensions produces four positions: drifters (inclusive and casual consumers), surfers (exclusive and casual consumers), exchangers (inclusive and intensive users) and clubbers (exclusive and intensive users). The drifters:

> had little awareness of their music consumer and producer practices even though their everyday life contexts regularly featured music within earshot. Music often played a minor role in these young people's everyday lives. Although music would be infrequently purchased or experienced in public contexts where high amounts of financial capital were necessary, its pervasive presence through casual media such as radio perhaps explains drifters' populist tastes and mainstream sensibilities.
>
> (Laughey 2006: 175)

The surfers, despite also being casual in consumption were exclusive in public practices – 'if specific types of music *texts* were immaterial to the pleasures of surfers, specific practices associated with exclusive music *contexts* were of paramount importance' (p. 177). Exchangers 'tended to invest more significance in mediated than co-present practices. Music texts and technologies would be more important to the everyday lives of exchangers than exclusive music contexts. Whilst exchangers' tastes would often be alternative and specific to particular music genres, their sensibilities leaned towards mainstream public practices of inclusion' (p. 177). Finally, 'clubbers engaged in intensive media use and exclusive public practices. Being a clubber refers more to a sense of membership in a specific music taste group than to the particular context of clubbing. However, the term is also apt because clubs were mainly perceived as sites for exclusive music consumption and production' (p. 178).

This typology is important for the attention to a range of different aspects of public and private, meaningful or casual interaction with music and other media. It is significant for the overall thrust of my argument as recognizing the significance of these different aspects, in the context of family, friends and individual meaning.

This sort of approach is also well represented in Lembo's (2000) book *Thinking Through Television*, where he convincingly argues that most previous theories and accounts of audiences and television are deficient. In terms of the arguments that I have set out in this book and chapter so far, there are two particularly important aspects to his argument. First, while having much admiration for the work done in cultural studies on audiences for television, he argues that it is limited by a continuing focus on issues of the power of television and the degree of audience resistance to it. In his account, this means that analysis has become overly focused on dimensions of audience response to the texts of television in these terms. This means that such analyses neglect what he sees as the more fully social aspects of how television is a part of what I have termed ordinary life. Therefore, second, a critical important part of his book is the call for an examination of the sociality of television viewing. As he says:

The more important issue, however, is whether or not we see power and resistance as *all* that is always already there in what people think and do; in my case, what they think and do with television. My own view is that, like power, sociality, too, is already there in the practices that comprise daily life, and, if cultural studies' analysts were to acknowledge this, then their understanding of power would be that much more sophisticated and complicated.

(Lembo 2000: 80–1)

His argument is that, in drawing on the insights of authors like Butler concerning the discursively performative nature of social life, but subjecting such focus on discourse to critique through the insights of interactionist sociologists like Goffman, a different type of understanding of the full sociality of television can be produced. This is a view and approach with which, it should be clear on the basis of the arguments of this book so far, I have much sympathy. Moreover, Lembo in part at least shows some of the complexities of the place of television through a very engaging consideration of the different degrees of mindfulness that is part of the practice of turning on the television in the evening. This both explores the varying levels of agency that are involved in this process and also shows how television is implicated in forms of everyday routine with respect to work, family interaction domestic responsibility, and so on.

Lembo, in my view, therefore captures a number of important themes that run through this book. However, there are some problems with his analysis, the consideration of which can contextualize the overall approach to be drawn from the discussion in this book. First, while his analysis usefully critiques aspects of previous approaches in pointing towards the need to consider sociability, as his own discussion progresses it becomes more like a rather conventional text audience study, which could have fitted into some of the discussions of the uses made of TV, and so on. In this respect, despite the overall aim, the more full understanding of social life around television is not achieved. Second, the analysis focuses on television. While this is justifiable in terms of the aims of the study, and by the fact that television is the most popular contemporary mass medium, it does mean that the roles of other cultural forms and the interactions between different media are not considered at any length. This is by no means a fault only of Lembo's work, as the recent tradition of audience studies has been dominated by the analysis of television. Third, the wider processes of cultural change that impinge on the processes of television sociability and provide a context through which they alter are little considered. This is a commonly expressed criticism of studies that focus on the micro-processes of everyday social interaction. In this respect the point is something of a cliché. However, it is important to recognize that there does need to be consideration of the way in which the wider social and cultural processes contextualize the way in which ordinary life is lived out. Finally, despite offering a significant critique of previous theorizations of the way in which audiences have been studied the theoretical approach that Lembo then uses is under-developed with respect to the overall nature of the evidence that he provides for the reader.

I make these points in this way, as it is important to recognize that the project that is represented by a book like Lembo's is, in my view, precisely the sort of direction that studies of media audiences should be taking. This is especially the case with the attention to the processes of sociability. In this sense the book serves to reveal important directions, especially combined with the overall approach to television and everyday life in the work of Silverstone (1994) that I considered at some length in an earlier chapter.

Conclusion

In this chapter, I have deepened the analysis of ordinary life to offer the context for why I see it as being constituted around processes of performing and audiencing. Thus, starting from the critique of previous understandings of media audience processes, I have expanded the scope of consideration to the diffused audience of ordinary life. This entails consideration of the increased interactions between simple, mass and diffused audiences, in a context where society and culture have become more spectacular and performative. The media fuel and are involved in the constitution of these processes. Moreover, these changes are themselves framed by the contextual processes outlined in Chapter 3. In addition there are different audience positions that can be taken up that involve different levels of commitment and enthusiasm. While this is another important step in my argument, it remains to show how this argument and approach can work out in further detail. This will involve more extensive discussion of the key processes that make up the ordinary processes of audiencing and performing. I have introduced these so far, especially in Chapter 2, as involving belonging, distinguishing and individualizing. These three dimensions relate to each other and are part of the wider processes. It is also important to remember that these processes themselves involve more specific aspects of ordinary life as I also briefly addressed in Chapter 2. Thus through the rest of the book, I will draw on specific studies of ordinary processes to substantiate some of the more general theoretical points. Some of this research I have carried out with various collaborators. The next chapter moves into this discussion with ideas of 'globalization and belonging'.

Note

1 My knowledge of Goffman has been greatly advanced by many conversations over the years with my colleague Greg Smith. Many thanks for these. For an overall discussion, see Smith (2006).

5 Globalizing, hybridizing *and* localizing: processes *of* elective belonging

In the previous chapter, I argued that ordinary life requires to be conceptualized in the context of the understanding of audience and performing processes. I concluded that these processes themselves involve belonging, distinguishing and individualizing and pursue these ideas (remembering the contexts and claims that I have outlined so far) over the next three chapters. In this chapter, I focus on belonging. I take my argument forward through the idea of 'elective belonging'. I will first of all introduce this concept and its context and then further contextualize it through processes of globalizing, before offering some illustrative evidence. I conclude by arguing that these processes can helpfully be theorized in the context of ideas of performance and audience, as scenic.

Belonging

Recent work has argued for a new approach to processes of belonging (Savage et al. 2005). This approach seeks to move away from accounts of belonging as somehow 'primordial' and therefore involving an inherent attachment to face-to-face community or as constructed through discourse and therefore without significant social anchoring. It sees belonging as a social process through which people evaluate a site of belonging in the context of their social trajectory and social and cultural positions. People construct and perform positions and identities that make them feel at home through processes of reflection, but also imaginings about themselves and others.

This argument develops themes from Bourdieu and reflects the influence of literatures that have evaluated the significance of Butler. In studying local belonging it is important to draw on:

> Bourdieu's interest in how people may feel comfortable or not in any one place, relating this to the habitus and capital of its residents. This allows us to explore local belonging as fluid and contingent, in a manner consistent with Probyn's (1996) and Fortier's (2000) insistence that belonging is not a given but is itself unstable, positing both states

(or unbelonging) from which one comes, and possible future states of belonging to which one may aspire.

(Savage et al. 2005: 11–12)

This approach builds on the arguments concerning spectacle, perform-ance and audience processes examined in the previous chapter, especially in exploring the diffused audience of ordinary life, focusing on the producing of belonging from local sites. Key aspects of this approach are captured in the term 'elective belonging', which seeks to combine modes of *agency* and the *processes* of belonging, that are affected by external forces (job moves, for example) and which are fluid. Furthermore: 'Belonging is not to a fixed community, with the implications of closed boundaries, but is more fluid seeing places as sites for *performing identities*' (Savage et al. 2005: 29, my emphasis).

The key here is the idea of performing (like the idea of belonging). This term draws attention to the audienced nature of these processes as theorized in Chapter 4 and further their (recursive) process-like nature. I therefore, wish to avoid the idea of the one-off event of 'performance', which is like a simple audience experience, or that of performativity, which can be theorized as a sophisticated IRP argument. The point is that performing encompasses a range of experiences that are sedimented aspects of ordinary life – in some respects like performativity (and the habitus) and the performance of the simple audi-ence experience. Performing as a key mechanism of elective belonging implies a degree of openness and contingency in social relations that other concepts discussed here have a tendency to close off. This is the case with performance, as it involves a one-off event, the subsequent effects of which are themselves variable, and performativity, as it involves a rather too closed circuit of ideo-logical incorporation and disputation.

The analysis of media and other ordinary experiences in diffused audi-ence terms via the ideas of belonging and performing therefore, I suggest, opens up a new terrain of analysis. Aspects of this are outlined in arguments such as that 'the media need to be understood in relation to the other dimen-sions of daily life, and connect to the meaning of place and imagination in crucial ways . . . Family life is played out in relation to television and cinema as much as it is with connection to schooling and membership of the PTA' (Savage et al. 2005: 179).

The point of this approach then shows how the routine aspects of media use, as articulated around the meanings of, for instance, concrete places, spaces, patterns of sociation and enthusiasm (what has often been theorized as fandom; see the discussion in Chapter 4 and Chapter 9) is part of the audiencing processes of the production via processes of performing that allow the development of elective belonging.

For example, an audience in a theatre, which is a good example of a simple audience, is framed by the diffused audience processes of ordinary life. Neither one nor the other of these experiences can be fully understood with-out reference to the other. Analysis may begin from either the experience of the theatre audience member in the theatre, thereby being very likely to raise wider issues of sociability, and so on, or it begins from the wider processes.

Overall, one mode of analysis is likely to suffer without the other. Similar points can be made with reference to the mass and diffused audiencing of cinema and a range of other cultural activities (Longhurst et al. 2007).

A similar sort of position can be derived from Butler but not in ways that she might have anticipated. Thus, in her discussion of drag in *Gender Trouble* (Butler 1999: 175), Butler argues that in drag, 'we are actually in the presence of three contingent dimensions of corporeality: anatomical sex, gender identity and gender performance' and further that 'we see sex and gender denaturalized by means of a performance which avows their directness and dramatizes the cultural mechanism of their fabricated unity'.

I think that the SPP does something similar for previous conceptions of the audience and ordinary life such as the bounded affected/responding groups of the individuals of the BPP and the incorporated/resistant groups of the IRP. These are reconfigured and rethought within the attention to the processes argued in the idea of the SPP. Thus to rewrite the quote from Butler, I would argue something along the following lines – I see the audiences of ordinary life as denaturalized by means of performing processes that avow their directness and dramatize the cultural mechanisms of their fabricated unity. It should be noted that this suggests some revision to the SPP. I would now wish to emphasize the importance of the idea of *performing* rather than performance (or indeed performativity) for the reasons outlined so far.

A number of processes of social life are part of and constitute the performance of elective belonging. These include decisions about where people choose to reside and therefore how they can build belonging on this basis, although residence should not be conflated with belonging. Examination of residential belonging involves consideration of the different meanings of places. This involves examination of other places that residents compared their place of residence to. It also entails discussion of the role of work and schooling for children in the generation of how people go about the processes of performing elective belonging. It also requires consideration of the way in which people use the media and how they imagine that they are cosmopolitan or local.[1]

Globalizing

Globalization processes have a number of different dimensions. First, it is important to recognize that 'the precise form and nature of global connections depends strongly on the precise field of practice that is being studied' (Savage et al. 2005: 207). Thus, mediated forms of practice like music and cinema had more spatial extension than residence. Global connections are uneven, but need to be traced in their specific patterns. Second, it should be restated that residential space is 'a key arena in which respondents define their social position' (p. 207). More specifically it can be argued that:

> The sorting processes by which people chose to live in certain places and others leave is at the heart of contemporary battles over social distinction. Rather than seeing wider social identities as arising out of the field

of employment it would be promising to examine their relationship to residential location. (p. 207)

Third, it should be reinforced that 'Places are defined not as historical residues of the local, or simply as sites where one happens to live, but as sites chosen by particular groups wishing to announce their identities . . . places offer visions of living which do not depend on the character of face-to-face relationships, or the historical character of the place' (p. 207). Fourth, while 'elective belonging involves people moving to a place and putting down roots' (p. 207), they also talk about other places that they know personally and through the media. Fifth, 'identities are developed through the networked geography of places articulated together' (p. 208).

These conclusions form the components of model of an alternative account of globalization that is specific, residential, mediatized concerned with identity and networked. Some of these arguments have already been considered at other points in this book. However, I have not theorized these interconnections. In much of the rest of this chapter, I do this via the idea of scene, arguing that performance of elective belonging is increasingly played out in a scenic manner.

Scenes

The concept of scene has been increasingly used to refer to sites of (predominantly) local music production and consumption. In some respects this has built on commonsense understandings of the idea as represented in ideas such as the Seattle scene or the Liverpool scene. Furthermore, at times the term has been used in conjunction with that of subculture, for example, in the work of Hodkinson (2002). There is much overlap in the literature in the use of these terms, although there has more often been an attempt to separate them (Hesmondhalgh 2005). In *Audiences* (Abercrombie and Longhurst 1998) we argued that the idea of scene offered a potential way forward for the study of the diffused audience and I take that argument forward here. This will require a brief recap before further development.

A key study that has advanced this research is that of Austin, Texas, by Barry Shank (1994). This study builds on earlier work by Shank and the sort of influential theorisation produced by Will Straw (1991: 373), who argues that the musical scene can be defined in the following way:

> That cultural space in which a range of musical practices co-exist, interacting with each other within a variety of processes of differentiation, and according to widely varying trajectories of change and cross-fertilization. The sense of purpose articulated within a musical community normally depends on an affective link between two terms: contemporary musical practices, on the one hand, and the musical heritage which is seen to render this contemporary activity appropriate to a given context, on the other. Within a music scene, that same sense of purpose is articulated within those forms of communication through which the building of musical alliances and the drawing of musical boundaries take place. The manner in which musical practices within the scene tie themselves

to processes of historical change occurring within a larger international musical culture will also be a significant basis of the way in which such forms are positioned within a scene at a local level.

Shank (1994) traces the development of the music scene in Austin, Texas, in some detail – filling in the way in which the different influences have come together to produce a changing musical patchwork. In more theoretical terms, Shank argues that the boundaries between producers and consumers break down in the sort of scene that is represented in Austin. Thus, as Shank argues 'within the fluid stream of potential meanings, the audience and the musicians together participate in a nonverbal dialogue about the significance of music and the construction of their selves' (p. 125). To develop and summarize this idea, Shank suggests that:

> Spectators become fans, fans become musicians, musicians are always already fans, all constructing the nonobjects of identification through their performances as subjects of enunciation – becoming and disseminating the subject-in-process of the signifying practice of rock 'n' roll music.
>
> (Shank 1994: 131)

This captures the way in which the participants in a scene can take on a number of different roles or can change their roles within it. This sort of change is also captured by Hodkinson (2002) in his study of Goth, where he shows how the Goth subculture can involve the promotion of gigs, tape swapping, the sale and purchase of clothing, and so on – suggesting the sort of fluidity and complexity of the construction of meaning theorized by Shank. It is illustrative that, in this context, Hodkinson often refers to the Goth scene.

Building on this sort of approach, where the idea of scene 'has increasingly been used as a model for academic research on the production, performance, and reception of popular music' (Peterson and Bennett 2004: 3), Peterson and Bennett (2004) identify three types of scene: local, translocal and virtual. Local scenes are those based around a particular place and has been the most common use made of the term. A local scene is:

> A focussed social activity that takes place in a delimited space and over a specific span of time in which clusters of producers, musicians, and fans realize their common musical taste, collectively distinguishing themselves from others by using music and other cultural signs often appropriated from other places, but recombined and developed in ways that come to represent the local scene. The focussed activity we are interested in here, of course, centers on a particular style of music, but such music scenes characteristically involve other diverse lifestyle elements as well. These usually include a distinctive style of dancing, a particular range of psychoactive drugs, style of dress, politics and the like.
>
> (Peterson and Bennett 2004: 8)

The translocal scene involves the communication between local scenes and it refers to 'widely scattered local scenes drawn into regular communication around a distinctive form of music and lifestyle' (Peterson and Bennett 2004: 6).

Examples of this sort of translocal scene given here include alternative rock in the 1980s, as examined by Kruse (1993) and the way in which hip-hop has diffused across the world, but taken on specific local forms. Another phenomenon discussed under this heading is the so-called 'music carnival' that existed around the American band The Grateful Dead, where 'a band's fans regularly follow their favorite musicians around the country from tour date to tour date and energize local devotees of the music and lifestyle' (Peterson and Bennett 2004: 10).

The virtual scene 'is a newly emergent formation in which people scattered across great physical spaces create the sense of scene via fanzines and, increasingly, through the internet' (pp. 6–7). As such technologies as the internet develop, it can be expected that there might be more virtual scenes developing. In their edited collection, Bennett and Peterson (2004) include a range of studies that they locate under these headings of local, translocal and virtual.

A problem with this expansion of the conceptualization of the idea of scene to include translocal and virtual is that it reduces the specificity of the concept and makes it descriptive rather than analytical. Thus, while it is useful to point out that scenes have translocal and virtual dimensions, I want to argue that it important to retain the idea that a scene involves some measure of potential co-present interaction. In terms initially theorized by Raymond Williams (1970), a scene involves a 'knowable community', even if the people involved in it can only 'imagine' that they can know each other. It seems likely that those who are enthusiastic about a form of music and a mode of dress will engage to differential degrees with others that live locally and who are involved as well as hoping to meet up with others that are involved but live elsewhere. The discussion of Goth by Hodkinson (2002) illuminates the differential interaction of these processes very well. In addition, Grazian's (2004) study of the blues scene in Chicago discusses the role of tourists in affecting the continuing existence of blues clubs, and so on.

There is a danger of loss of specificity and purchase once the concept of scene is generalized unless the particular features to which it draws attention – the aspect of interaction around some degree of performance, the role of place in acting as a node of communication – are recognized and retained. Building on this approach, therefore, I elaborate three general arguments in the rest of this chapter. First, the idea of scene does not just apply to music-based connections that are located in space. Given that there are increasing modes of media convergence, and that music is often related to a range of other activities and places, I see no argument for suggesting *a priori* why music should be the prime way of conceptualizing a scene. Second, I wish to retain a focus on place as a key determinant of what a scene is. However, I do this in a context forged by the arguments made concerning 'elective belonging' that have been introduced in this chapter so far. Place is not conceptualized as belonging to a local community or having a 'structure of feeling' but as somewhere where elective belonging, and the identities that it forges, is lived out via different modes of performance. Third, I will suggest that a scene in the sense that I will define it is like a scene in a performed narrative on the stage. The scene is a short period of a narrative that may involve a number of characters in significant interaction. It is related to the overall narrative and helps to move that narrative along, but itself only makes sense in the context of the overall narrative. A scene is both temporal and spatial and thus enables the bringing together of ideas of narrative, media, interaction and performance in audienced processes lived out through modes of belonging.

Beyond music

I have already suggested that scene does not have to refer only to musical production and consumption in place. Thus, Straw argues that:

> The term 'scene' has represented one attempt to characterize the informal sorts of social organization that have taken shape around particular cultural practices. Writers typically have recourse to 'scene' when the activities being described encompass cultural roles that extend beyond (or blur the lines between) those of either performer or audience, and when the relationships between individuals involved in cultural practices offer some combination of the formal and informal.
>
> (Straw 2003: 349)

This application of this sort of argument specifically to popular music is justified by Straw on the following grounds:

> If the term 'scene' has seemed particularly pertinent to the analysis of popular music, this has been, in part, because – compared, for example, to the fields of film and television creation – a wide range of musical activities can be found between the purely professional level of the international music industry and the sorts of amateur and quasi amateur practices that are to be found in any locale.
>
> (Straw 2003: 349)

This is an argument also made by Cohen in her discussion of scene. She argues that:

> The concept of scene is in some ways particularly pertinent to popular music. Popular music scenes develop because local amateur music making is cheaper and more accessible and extensive than many other types of local cultural production, such as film and television, and they are also particularly geographically mobile. Musicians and audiences travel and tour on a regular basis, music products are widely distributed in the form of CDs, tapes, fanzines, and so on, and music sounds and discussions are broadcast on radio and television and via the internet.
>
> (Cohen 1999: 248)

These arguments have a degree of plausibility, as on the face of it the comparison of music production to that of film and television does suggest differences of scale. However, technological change and change in cultural and social relations have narrowed this gap in important ways. First, as discussed in the literature on fans, people are involved in cultural production on the ground with the texts of film and television that insert new practices into areas outside that of the international film and television area. Consumers have to some degree become producers. Second, and more significantly for this part of the argument, technological innovation is enabling the transfer of practices that once were the province of professionals and had high equipment costs to ordinary life. Thus, while the history of the development of photography as a 'vernacular practice' is well known, this process has reached a new stage when it is possible to take photographs on a mobile phone and transmit them easily to friends and family. Likewise, the development of relatively inexpensive digital cameras and camcorders has facilitated the recording of ordinary life. It is very common for an event or, say, a school concert to be recorded by the majority of the audience. These recordings might then be transmitted to others so that those, for example friends and family, who are living elsewhere, can view these activities via their computers.

Media are therefore becoming interactive in ways that move film and TV production closer to the everydayness of TV. These sorts of process are also being facilitated by the availability of hardware and software for media production in schools and colleges. While these processes are uneven, the growth of subjects such as media studies and forms of digital production can lead to modes of amateur production that can be seen as essentially similar to that of music. This is reinforced by the way in which the boundaries between these forms are being blurred; with, for example, mobile phones and mp3 players facilitating everyday production and consumption around a range of increasingly integrated media.

There is a danger of being overenthusiastic about these shifts, of being technologically determinist and of overestimating the extent of their occurrence. However, despite this I argue that these shifts undermine the case for confining the term scene to music-based ideas of place.

Place

I suggest that the extension of the idea of scene to cover modes of more widespread interaction has been done on the basis of misconceived response to the processes of globalization. Indeed, even the earlier theorizations of the concept sought to address this issue. Thus, Straw (2003) characterizes his earlier (1991) conceptualization in the following way:

> Straw's rethinking of the notion of 'scene' was devised to intervene against a perceived over-valorization of the sorts of musical localism common within alternative rock scenes in North America in the late 1980s. While the small-scale, artisanal character of musical activity in a multitude of local scenes made this activity seem more firmly grounded than many others in local identities, Straw argues that the culture of alternative rock was a highly cosmopolitan one. From one locale to another, a relatively similar range of styles and practices had been replicated, suggesting that an analysis of this activity might be full of lessons about musical cosmopolitanism and globalization as it was about the persistence or resurgence of specifically local identities and values.
>
> (Straw 2003: 350)

In a similar way, Cohen argues that 'efforts have been made to reconceptualize scenes in order to shift emphasis from music as local culture to music as global, mobile culture' (1999: 243). While there is nothing wrong with this sort of move and indeed it clearly needs to be made, I suggest that the point is to recognize the points made about globalization and cosmopolitanism earlier in this chapter, earlier in this book and in the arguments in *Globalization and Belonging* (Savage et al. 2005). What matters in my argument is the living out of globalizing processes and how cosmopolitanism is patterned through particular activities. This is the basis for the critique of the rather static versions of local community that are mounted in *Globalization and Belonging*. Thus, it is important, I suggest, to emphasize the changing nature of the scenes where elective belonging takes place. I argue later that this is one of the most specific benefits of the concept.

Scene and narrative

A relatively neglected aspect of the concept of scene is to see that scene is a fairly short period in the overall performance of a narrative. Thus, a scene in a play, while it may be short or long, is only a part of the *overall* action. I will develop this point further later, but at the moment comment on how this might work with respect to the musical conceptions of scene examined so far. Thus, while a scene may be based in one place and may take place over a period of time, it will have limitations that need to be recognized. Some scenes will be relatively short and specific, thus there is little talk today of a 'Coventry' scene, as this was restricted to the brief period of success of two-tone music of the late 1970s and early 1980s. By contrast, Shank's (1994) consideration of Austin, Texas, traces the mutation of the scene over a period of time. I want to argue that we can see these periods as points and stages in the overall evolution of how the narrative of a place is performed and audienced. Thus, it may be best to think of this as the performance of a number of scenes over a period of time.

Problems with scene

So far I have argued that scene is both an important concept and one that can have purchase beyond specifically musical scenes. I will conclude the chapter with further development of that argument. However, before I do that I consider arguments against the idea of scene. In particular, I shall examine the important points made by Hesmondhalgh (2005). Like other writers, Hesmondhalgh focuses on musical scenes and in particular on the way that scene has been used by some to theorize the links between young people and popular music and therefore (along with other concepts such as *tribe* and *neo-tribe*) to replace the idea of subculture. This argument is significant, but it is not as relevant to my purposes here as Hesmondhalgh's potentially significant criticisms of the concept of scene itself. A core aspect of this is his argument that 'scene is a confusing term. It suggests a bounded place but has also been used to refer to more complex spatial flows of musical affiliation; the two major ways in which the term is used are incompatible with each other' (2005: 23). Moreover, Hesmondhalgh further argues that the two major theoretical sources for the idea of scene (the work of Straw and Shank) discussed earlier are very different, if not incompatible. Thus:

> Whereas Straw shows a Bourdieu-ian concern with processes of legitim-ation and the competition for cultural prestige, and looks upon musical practices from a distance, so to speak, Shank is working within a frame-work that draws a contrast between these transformative practices and the dominant or mainstream culture. More fundamentally still, Straw seems to be advocating scene as a word that questions the notion of local community that Shank celebrates, and which Straw associates specifically with the rock genre.
>
> (Hesmondhalgh 2005: 28)

Indeed, Shank's formulation is influenced by forms of psychoanalysis that do not figure in Straw's account at all. Hesmondhalgh recognizes that these differences can be seen as part of a productive contradiction in the idea of scene, but ultimately sees that this makes the idea unstable, especially when it is used to replace the idea of subculture. To advance this discussion Hesmond-halgh considers some further work on scene by Straw (2001). He argues that for Straw the benefit of scene is it can capture some of the fuzziness of boundaries and that it can detach practices in place from too rigid ideas of subculture and class, while offering the promise that it can be reconnected to these variables. Most significantly Hesmondhalgh argues as follows in quoting Straw:

> Finally, Straw observes that ' "scene" seems able to evoke both the cozy intimacy of community and the fluid cosmopolitanism of urban life. To the former, it adds a sense of dynamism: to the latter, a recognition of the inner circles and weighty histories which give each seemingly fluid sur-face a secret order' (Straw 2001, p. 248). But how does the term achieve this metaphorical work? Of course, analytical concepts work via meta-phor and association (think of Bourdieu's field, or Habermas's public sphere) but in my view scene has gone beyond the point where such metaphorical associations can aid in the analysis of spatial dimensions of popular music. The term has been used for too long in too many different and imprecise ways for those involved in popular music studies to be sure that it can register the ambivalences that Straw hopes that it will.
>
> (Hesmondhalgh 2005: 30)

I am not convinced, ultimately, by Hesmondhalgh's critique, as I tend to agree that scene can encompass ideas of intimacy and cosmopolitanism via the more precise theorizations of elective belonging and that the theoriza-tion of performance and audiencing actually does the theoretical work that Hesmondhalgh suggests is necessary. In this way, Hesmondhalgh's points suggest not so much the abandonment of the idea of scene as its further theorization in a different context, which is my most important overall point.

Scene, performing, audiencing and elective belonging

My argument is that the spaces of elective belonging can be conceptualized as scenes. I suggest that there are a number of potential benefits of such a theorization. I repeat the point that I am not simply adopting a Goffman-like analogy of life as dramatic, although aspects of that theorization have increasingly influenced the point of view here. The key point is to see the spaces of elective belonging as media drenched and involving new interactions influenced by globalizing processes. However, certain aspects of a Goffmanian approach have significance. This is also the sort of approach taken to the study of youth cultural interaction around popular music taken by Laughey (2006) and can inform the sort of study of sport undertaken by Crawford (2004).

A key aspect of the idea of scene as I use it is to point to the way in which a range of media interact with other aspects of social and cultural life to produce ways of belonging that involve active choices. Thus, the following from Cohen (1999) can be generalized beyond popular music to characterize a scene in general:

> Reasons for getting involved with music-making include the fact that it offers them: a particular lifestyle; a social network and identity outside of work, family, or home; a sense of purpose, status, and prestige; a unique means of communicating emotion and idea; and the lure of artistic and financial success.
>
> (Cohen 1999: 240)

In studying places of elective belonging as scenes, the particular scenes are seen as a stage in the wider and long-run narrative of the place and those who elect to live there. A scene can therefore be thought of as an episode in the longer run narrative, much like the narrative of, say, a television soap opera. There is no controlling author of this narrative, or indeed the scene, rather the social actors involved are the authors of the scene, as contextualized by wider general factors.

The scene involves those who are performing the processes of elective belonging, but, in contrast to the theatre, the audience is also part of the scene itself. Thus, while in some circumstances the audience aspect of the process of the scene will be dominant (as in when people are constituted as a simple audience in the theatre or at a sports event); in many others performance and audience aspects are blurred and conjoined. It is important to recognize that these are processes and that, therefore, belonging is a process that involves performing and audiencing. This is particularly significant as it means that elective belonging can involve feelings of belonging more at certain points than at others. Elective belonging can therefore be unevenly distributed and some may feel that they do not belong where they are currently living. In this sense that scene has changed in ways that make some people unhappy within the overall narrative of belonging.

Scenes are media drenched and involve social networks and a range of practical activities. The scene involves a varying number of social actors, some of whom will be known to each other, but the overwhelming number will be imagined or thought of as potentially knowable. These social actors will have a range of different identities and to push the analogy further, these can be seen as involving them as adopting different characters in different contexts, or that character, and hence identity, has assumed a measure of fluidity that means that people are adaptable in different contexts. While the current sociological truisms about such fluidity of identity (usually derived from readings of authors such as Bauman and Giddens) are problematic when not backed up by evidence from empirical and substantive research, they have been shown to have validity in complex ways in such study. Aspects of this have already been considered, but the next chapter will address some of the key issues, primarily through discussion of contemporary class identities. The fact that scenes involve people as characters means that identities have mask-like qualities. This has been an issue much discussed in the literature that derives from the work on Butler, where ideas of performance and drag have been considered in some detail. While, on the one hand, there is a danger that some of the discussion here is both constrained by the paradigm of incorporation and resistance or, on the other, implying that the process of identity construction is completely voluntaristic, it is my contention that such processes are increasing sedimenting into a range of aspects of ordinary life.

It possible to say that some scenes are livelier than others. Thus, for example, based on interviews with young people, Laughey contrasts the music scene in Carlisle, often seen as a relatively isolated town in the north-west of England close to the border with Scotland, with that in the city of Manchester. He describes Carlisle as a 'community' in contrast to the 'scene' of Manchester: 'Although Carlisle might still be conceived to have a music scene, it is a homogeneous and static scene compared to the fluid, transient scene or scenes that interact and vie for supremacy in Manchester' (Laughey 2006: 191). However, in contrast to this distinction, I argue that Carlisle is just as scenic as Manchester in the terms that I have discussed here. It may be that Carlisle is thought by some to be less interesting than Manchester, but this is open to debate. In the same way that an experimental play is still a play, as is one by, say, Noël Coward, a place will have scenic processes of elective belonging, as will another. They are simply different.

This can be illustrated by the differences between the places that we studied in the research that forms the basis for *Globalization and Belonging* (Savage et al. 2005). While they are all areas of broadly middle-class culture that has a degree of ordinariness, they exhibit many cultural and social differences. This is not the place to repeat those differences (see Savage et al. 2004a, 2004b in addition), but it can be recognized that different processes (as well as in some cases similar) processes of elective belonging are performed in each place. In all cases the media are playing a significant role. As we argued in that book:

> Compared to people's concerns with their choice of residence, their schooling, and the kinds of places which they aspired to, there is no doubt that media use allows significantly more spatial and social diversity for our audiences . . . We have emphasised the way that it permits the elaboration of an ordinary culture which has widely shared cultural referents in all places.
>
> (Savage et al. 2005: 179)

It is possible to add to this that the conceptualization of these places as scenes allows further understanding of the processes of audiencing and performing that take place in the processes of elective belonging.

Conclusion

In this chapter, I have extended the consideration of elective belonging in the context of the themes of this book so far. To recap, this means attention to the contextualized processes of ordinary life, where audiencing and performing are critical. Belonging is one of the key aspects of ordinary life conceived in these terms. Elective belonging can therefore be seen as a significant concept as it enables consideration of choices that people make in their ordinary lives in the flow of wider processes. Thus, we belong to places and feel attachments to people, things and processes and so on to differential degrees. These are not once and for all but change over time. Moroever, these attachments take place in an increasingly globalized world, where the media are of increased significance. Attachments and modes of belonging are lived through globalized and mediatized processes. The mediatized processes are uneven as people have different degrees of exposure to them and differential attachments, but they play out in belonging. An important way therefore to bring together these processes is through the concept of scene, which increasingly considers the relation between the global and the local in a mediatized world. In addition, it can be located within the core ideas of performing and audiencing of this book. The next step in my argument is to consider these ideas of performing in the context of the relationship between wider social and cultural processes and the identity of individuals.

Note

1 In addition to the book-length study, we have developed the analysis through a number of published papers on class (Savage et al. 2001), the different forms of belonging in the places studied (Savage et al. 2004a, 2004b), parent teacher associations and schooling (Bagnall et al. 2003), media use (Longhurst et al. 2001, 2007) and museum visiting (Longhurst et al. 2004).

6 Imagining, performing *and* identifying: class, identity *and* culture

In the previous two chapters, I have extended the analysis of the spectacle/performance paradigm in a number of ways. Drawing on theories of performing and belonging, I have sought to consider how attachments are produced in space and time. The media are important to these processes in the ways that I have foregrounded. In this chapter, I want to take this approach further through examination of contemporary work on class, culture and identity. In the first instance, this may seem like an unusual move to make, as class has tended to be thought of as redundant in the development of many of the accounts and theories of cultural and social change that I have considered in this book so far. However, as I have argued earlier, the relative divorce between sociology and media/cultural studies has acted as a block to better understanding of these processes. I argue, following a number of recent authors, that this is problematic. There are several reasons why this is so. First, as has been shown, forms of social inequality and social division that are broadly class related are still pertinent to society today. Class in this sense is alive if not something that we should see as 'well'. However, an understanding of class that is divorced from the arguments that I have advanced so far is itself weakened. Second, as I will show, there have been several moves in class analysis, that have the potential significantly to contribute to the theorization of culture and ordinary life as outlined so far. These theorizations have also added much to the theorization of the concept of identity. There is a danger that work in cultural theory, cultural studies and media studies on performance and audiences does not pay this work sufficient attention as class is somehow seen to be an 'old-fashioned' idea. It will be shown that the parameters of class analysis are indeed changing (and being changed) in a number of important ways, which contribute to the development of the approach to cultural change and ordinary life that I am proposing in this book. In particular then, I read this work on class through the lens of the arguments so far and for what these approaches tell us about the changing nature of the social and cultural imagination, how identities are performed (or are not performed) and how this relates to the ideas of audiencing and belonging that form the core of this book.

I will develop my analysis through several stages. I begin by setting out the argument for a renewed class analysis. This will lead me to a more expansive consideration of the work of Skeggs (2004) as this facilitates my formulation of a further consideration of a number of ideas of identity. This will be followed by a similar consideration of the work of Sayer (2005) for the same reasons. One further introductory comment is necessary. In developing my argument in this chapter through a focus on class, I do not seek to downplay other equally significant forms of social division and inequality. Rather, first, I would argue that the sort of approach that is being considered here has more often been considered in the light of such divisions of gender and race. In this sense, class can be seen as a kind of 'limit' case. If the argument works here, then it is all the more powerful as class divisions and class identities have often been seen as stable and in some sense 'traditional'. Second, as will be seen, these modes of social division actually influence one another in a number of important ways and to consider class often actually means paying different forms of attention to these other forms of inequality as bases for identity formation anyway.

Class, culture and identity: a new agenda

A number of writers have argued recently that there is a new approach to the analysis of class. I will take a paper by Devine and Savage (2005) to exemplify key aspects of this approach, although as with all new developments there are actually different points of emphasis by a number of the authors involved and some that are debating the position suggest that indeed this position might not be as new as some of its advocates suggest (Crompton and Scott 2005).

Devine and Savage (2005) make a number of important points. First, it is important to recognize that while there has been a renewed attention to the ideas of culture and identity within class analysis in the contemporary period, such attention has been an important aspect of that analysis. Thus, 'rather than seeing the issue of culture as a new one, we concur with Abbott (2001) that it has always been one of the core concerns in the discipline' (2005: 3). However, despite this significant presence class and culture were considered in a particular way within sociological research, especially within Marxist class analysis, but in other variants as well, 'studies were organised around a "class formation problematic" that examined the ways that people might be aware of their structural class position' (p. 5). This involved a particular understanding of the relationship between structure and culture, which, following Pahl (1989), Devine and Savage (2005) call a 'S-C-A [i.e. structure–culture–action] approach'. Here 'researchers saw consciousness as the intermediary between structure and action' (p. 5). This became the terrain for debate in much British class analysis in the 1960s and 1970s. The debate was about the nature of these links, whether they existed or indeed were dissolving due to wider changes in society. One of the problems was that there was a 'need for a more complex understanding of the relationship between class and culture' (p. 8). There were effectively two ways out of this situation. The first involved an ever more complex measurement of structural or 'objective' class locations or positions using increasingly sophisticated quantitative techniques. This was combined with a view of the culture problem that theorized links between structure and action via a rational action model (RAT). The issues with the sort of approach are considered further in Chapter 7, where I draw extensively on other work by Devine (especially Devine 2004). In Devine and Savage's (2005) view this sort of response 'is very much a minority concern within the discipline as a whole, and the dominant approach has been to adopt the view that taking culture seriously involves breaking from stratification research, at least as conventionally understood' (p. 11). However, Devine and Savage suggest that a different approach is both possible and necessary. This means not following reductive models of class culture and identity, but also and, very importantly, not suggesting an end to class analysis either.

They argue 'once class-consciousness is not seen as a "reflex" of class position, it can be studied in a variety of more innovative ways' (p. 12). A key part of this shift is a renewed emphasis on class and identity. They suggest that this move can be found in the work of a number of writers and that three themes have run through this new agenda. The first is methodological in that there has been a shift from quantitative to qualitative methods in the study of class, as this 'allows a much fuller account of the nuances of class identifications' (p. 12). Second, and very important in the overall context of this book, is 'a concern to place awareness in context of people's everyday lives, rather than to relate it to abstract expectations of what class awareness should be, or even might be, like' (p. 12), which chimes exceptionally well with the project of this book for the analysis of mediatized ordinary life. Third, there is:

> A common awareness that the complexities and ambivalences of class awareness should be analysed in their own terms, rather than as a difficulty to be explained away whether this be through recourse to a dominant ideology, organizational forms, or whatever. This has led to an interest in thinking through how the ambivalences and complexities of popular identities and forms of awareness can be understood.
>
> (Devine and Savage 2005: 13)

For Devine and Savage, this leads to an emphasis on the work of Bourdieu, as the interconnections between his concepts of habitus, capitals and fields produces a conceptual armoury that 'points towards a different kind of approach to culture and subjectivity than in older forms of class analysis' (p. 14). I have discussed these aspects of Bourdieu's work earlier in this book and consider the significance of his ideas of capital further in the next chapter. Thus it is possible to consider straightaway how more specifically Devine and Savage suggest that this theory represents an advance for class theory and research. There are four points that they emphasize:

First, in contrast to earlier approaches which 'see awareness as linked to self-recognition of one's position in the system, an ability to name your social location', Bourdieu's position 'is consistent with a structuralist or post-structuralist theory of language which means that identification, for Bourdieu, is not based on recognising oneself as belonging to a given position, but as differentiating oneself from others in a field' (Devine and Savage 2005: 14). While this may suggest that awareness is like a game with conscious tactics, which in some respects it may be, though these sorts of metaphor can be overextended in social and cultural analysis. There is an issue of intent here, but despite this issue there can be renewed attention to the fluidity of class identities.

Second, in approaches influenced by Bourdieu, identity is relational and identity claims affect the nature of a field or fields: 'Becoming conscious of one's position in a field actually can make the stakes of that field more compelling and powerful so actually reinforcing the legitimacy of the field itself' (Devine and Savage 2005: 14). Furthermore, 'claims to recognition are claims by subordinate groups to be taken as agents within a field, and can have the paradoxical effect of validating the rules of the game as a whole' (p. 14). Thus, identity is relational in important ways (as well as relatively fluid) and 'moves' to claim particular identities can have the effect of reinforcing the 'rules of the game' that may be defining those making the move in ways that reinforce their subordination.

Third, Bourdieu's approach suggests fluidity in a different way. He works with a variety of fields, 'with no clear pre-determined relationship between them, with the result that his account is more fluid and attentive to change and the power of agency. Insofar as fields are inter-related, this depends on the activities of dominant classes who are able to traverse different fields more easily than those whose stakes are confined to fewer fields' (p. 15).

Fourth, Bourdieu suggests a different kind of reflexivity: 'As people move between fields they become aware of the different kinds of stakes that exist in diverse fields, and hence can become more reflexive about the kinds of tactics they can pursue' (p. 15). While this may suggest that people become free to change their identities and develop them on the basis of this sort of process, there is a very significant rider, in that some people are freer in this than others.

> The ability to move between fields is itself variable and dependent on particular kinds of habitus that support mobile personality characteristics, personal flexibility, and so on. It is those with stakes in many fields, namely male members of dominant social classes, who thereby find it easier to develop various kinds of reflexivity (Devine and Savage 2005: 15).

Bourdieu's account is therefore important in that it facilitates a more complex understanding of the fluidity, relational nature and reflexivity of identities, but with an emphasis on the point that this is not something that all people are free to engage in to the same extent. Such 'freedom' or lack of it will be affected by a contingent interplay between habitus, capital and field. Importantly, there are particular activities, fields and habituses that are more legitimate than others. While this suggests itself as a powerful agenda there are some problems. Savage and Devine raise four in particular:

First, it may be that Bourdieu's account allows less fluidity than some writers in this new class agenda would suggest. In the end, it may be that the objective power of structural forces means that people in the end submit. For Savage and Devine, the work of Skeggs (1997) on the culture and identifications of a group of working-class women has a tendency to 'read popular culture as a form of false consciousness' (p. 16), which implies that there is some 'true consciousness' to be found. I will consider some more recent arguments from Skeggs in this light later, especially in the context of the points that I have made about the work of Butler in the examination of the idea of performativity. However, a further aspect of this point is also significant as it means being 'more attentive to the positive virtues of working-class cultural forms' (p. 16). This is significant, but it can be extended to consider the virtues of a range of 'devalued' cultural practices, not just those that rather narrowly might be seen to be associated with the working class. Thus, in Chapter 9, I consider the idea of enthusing, partly to continue this attention to forms of culture that tend to be devalued. Moreover, it is important to remember that what it is to be working class is defined culturally in a number of ways. It is not just that certain forms of culture are associated with this group.

Second, for Devine and Savage, 'the relationship between discursive and more practical forms of awareness remains unclear' (2005: 16). They ask a pertinent question of 'how do people's actual elaborate identities relate to the complexities of their everyday lives, and how is it possible for these identities to take more critical forms?' (p. 16). Can only social scientists really see through the forest of everyday (or ordinary) life to see exploitative relations and ways out of them? This is a perennial issue that involves, I would argue, paying detailed attention to the complexities of ordinary life in the way theorized here.

Third, it may be argued that Devine and Savage suggest that Bourdieu's theory retains ideas of society as bounded especially in national terms, in ways that much contemporary sociology has questioned. These approaches emphasize the interconnections between global flows and the mobilities of people and objects as well as identities. However, one argument is that it is possible to consider the way in which identity is both mobile and attached to place, as the consideration of 'elective belonging' earlier in this book suggested. I also pick up this point further later. While Devine and Savage seem rather agnostic on the benefits of Bourdieu's approach in this context, I would suggest that they are being unduly pessimistic.

Fourth, there is a methodological point. As they point out, 'Bourdieu's own research practice has been subject to criticism, for instance in its naïve use of personal testimonies in *The Weight of the World* [1999b]' (p. 17). As they suggest, the new forms of class analysis are working with a variety of methods. This has in my view much to recommend it. However, Devine and Savage strike again a somewhat pessimistic or defensive note when they say that, 'whilst we now have a clear sense of the limitations of the "employment aggregate approach", it is unclear how to develop an alternative' (p. 17). In my view it is not necessary to seek to develop one alternative, and class (and other modes of analysis) will actually be the stronger for the use of different methods with respect to different modes of analysis. It may be that such methods show up different processes and that these then require further consideration and debate. Thus, as will be considered at greater length in Chapter 8, the idea of the cultural omnivore can be examined in quantitative and qualitative ways to illuminating effect.

While there are therefore some potential riders that need to be placed on an overenthusiastic endorsement of Bourdieu's account, it does provide new and alternative ways of thinking of class, culture and identity. I will offer some other potential issues later. However, it is worth considering further one specific study that Devine and Savage locate in this framework. Anthias (2005) considers what she terms the 'intersectionality' model of social divisions, where 'forms of inequality and subordination are distinctive yet interlocking' (p. 36). While this might be contentious for older forms of class analysis or what she terms the 'reductionist' model, there is, in my mind, not much to dispute here. This can in many respects, I would argue, be taken as a safe ground. However, as Anthias suggests, it is important to move this sort of account from the descriptive to the more theoretical. She does this via a discussion of the 'identity' model. This has been an increasingly common account and the approach that I have considered so far in this chapter has made much of the idea of identity as has been set out. Anthias mounts a critique of what I would see as some forms of this sort of approach. Indeed she makes two potentially important criticisms of this idea:

> First, the concept has been expanded so much that it has lost its specificity, so it can embrace everything, for example, when shifting or multiple notions are used to correct the essentialising of earlier concepts. Secondly, the concept always takes us back to the theoretical baggage about communal identity as generic and fundamental in social processes. Whilst acknowledging that people's notions of belonging are important social facts, we cannot presuppose that they are always necessary or determining elements in collective placement or action.
>
> (Anthias 2005: 39)

While, on the face of it, these are potentially significant points, it is not clear that they represent a critique of the concept of identity itself, rather than of particular uses of it and the slippages that are involved. That is to say this is not a necessary implication of the concept itself. This seems to be the case when the important way in which she develops her argument is considered. This involves attention to ideas of belonging. ' "Where do I belong?" is a recurrent thought, however, for most of us. Asking this question is usually prompted by a feeling that there are a range of spaces, places, locales and identities that we do not and cannot belong to' (Anthias 2005: 39). Thus in rejecting a form of identity approach it is possible to retain an emphasis on the issues that a sociological attention to processes of identity suggest and to divorce this attention from particular modes of identity politics. Thus, Anthias proposes that focus should fall on 'narratives of location' and positionality: 'A narrative is an account that tells a story and a narrative of location, as it is used here, is an account that tells a story about how we place ourselves in terms of social categories, such as those of gender, ethnicity and class at a specific point in time and space' (p. 42). It is further important to recognize that such narratives involve 'a rejection of what one is not rather than a clear and unambiguous formulation of what one is' (p. 43). These are points that inform the idea of elective belonging and, moreover, some of the other arguments of this book, as:

The narrative constitutes a means for understanding the ways in which the narrator at a specific point in time and space is able to make sense and articulate their placement in the social order of things. This, however, also means the recognition of the narrative as an action, as a performance.

(Anthias 2005: 43)

This is a very important emphasis, although, in common with my earlier discussion, I wish to suggest that the idea of performance here should be replaced with that of performing and audiencing, in particular to capture the processual aspect. Narratives of location are important ways of performing belonging to some things and disassociating from others. This is significantly to do with the fact that performing involves audiencing as well and that the intertwining of these processes has made the different dimensions of narration clearer. This leads to further aspects of identity, but this is predicated on considering in addition to the points from Devine and Savage, some other potentially problematic aspects of Bourdieu.

There are three key issues. First, there is a danger that the emphasis on fields and the strategies and tactics of social actors within fields leads to a representation of social life as a kind of game. While there is a long tradition of considering social life through such theories and the accounts that they produce, there are also difficulties. Especially important is the point that it is possible on quite basic levels for an individual to decide whether or not to join in a game. While this is transferable to social life in that we can decide whether to engage in one activity rather than another, and we can decide whether to participate in some fields and not others, our choices are subject to considerable restraint. Of course, this is one of the strengths of examining fields relative to the different forms of capital, which affect movement across them.

The second point is connected, as there is a possibility that the work inspired by Bourdieu can slip into a voluntarism that overestimates the degree to which people have freedom to construct identities, forms of culture and modes of belonging. For example, it might be the case that this sort of point can be made against the idea of 'elective belonging' that I have discussed elsewhere in this book. Thus it might be argued that this implies that anyone can elect to belong to groups or to belong to places and so on. Of course, this is not the case as again a range of social and cultural processes limit such freedoms. However, this should not be used to devalue the concept itself, as these 'constraints' are recognized in it. However, I suggest that this is rather a 'risk factor' that needs to be kept in view when such concepts are deployed.

Third, there are issues with the 'capital' model as it can infer that all social life is conducted according to economic-type processes. An example of this could be an idea that people are spending all their time considering how to invest or deploy their various capital assets. Or that they are seeking ways to secure those modes of capital that they do not possess but would like to. There is some danger of these ideas shading into a version of rational action theory (RAT), which sees social and cultural life in related calculative terms and which downplays other dimensions of cultural life. This is a particular danger that is considered in the work of Skeggs (2004), which also has much to say on some of the other potential dangers (although they are not expressed in quite the same terms I have outlined) discussed here. This is significant work on a number of levels for the arguments in this chapter and for the wider argument of the book and I now turn to it.

Inscription, exchange, value and perspective

In accord with the general approach outlined in this chapter so far, a key aspect of Skeggs' work has involved taking culture seriously in the reconsideration of class. As with the other authors considered, this does not involve a return to earlier models, but rather entails the deployment of a number of strands in contemporary feminist, cultural and social theory to retheorize processes of class making, characterization and exclusion. A key strand in her work is an opposition to those contemporary and social theories that in her view overemphasize mobility and the pliability of cultures and identities. This is characterized as a middle-class, academic view that, due to the influences of its own social location, fails to see the processes to which, for example, the working class continue to be marked. I comment further on this view later. Skeggs' work covers much ground and I will focus on three main aspects of it, which are of particular use for my argument. First, I will outline rather briefly the key overall nature of her approach. Second, I discuss the limitations of the capital and exchange ideas that she identifies. Third, and most importantly, I consider at greater length the account of contemporary identity that she deploys. This will have implications for my own theorization of this, especially as considered in Chapter 9.

As Skeggs says: 'The way some cultural characteristics fix some groups and enable others to be mobile will be a central exploration of this book' (2004: 1). Thus, the advantages, especially of some middle-class groups in mobility, suggest that other members of society will be disadvantaged. Of course, there are other forms of mobility – such as migrant labour – that are not always advantaged by mobility. However, in broad terms Skeggs' emphasis can be followed. She suggests that four key processes underlie and run through the argument of her book. These are inscription, exchange, evaluation and perspective. To begin the discussion of these terms, consider Skeggs' description (2004: 2):

> First, how do certain bodies become *inscribed* and then marked with certain characteristics? Second, what *systems of exchange* enable some characteristics to be read as good, bad, worthy and unworthy? Thus, how is *value attributed, accrued, institutionalized and lost* in the process of exchange? And how is this value both *moral and economic*? Third, how is value produced through different *perspectives* (different ways of knowing, hearing and seeing that represent particular interests)? Fourth, we need to know how these systems of inscription, exchange, valuing, institutionalization and perspective provide the condition of possibility for being *read by others in the relationships* that are formed by groups; what are its effects?

An important set of emphases derive from this analysis. Thus, in putting a particular mode of emphasis on exchange, and combining this with how inscription works, Skeggs argues that she is able to see 'the way that value is transferred onto bodies and read off them and the mechanisms by which it is retained, accumulated, lost or appropriated' (p.13). This involves a wider understanding of the idea of exchange in the context of the sort of consideration of Bourdieu outlined earlier.

Skeggs develops an extended analysis of how concepts like exchange and market have developed historically. The detail of this discussion is outwith the specific concerns of this book. However, it is important to note that her analysis shows first that such terms are not 'neutral', that is they are not free from social context and social content, but moreover they are performative in the sense already considered earlier in this book. That is they bring into existence that which they name through the act (performance) of speaking (for an audience). Moreover, in Skeggs' analysis such processes are those that mark class, even if class is not directly named. 'When we come across the terms economic, social body, exchange, market, self, interest, rational action, abstract space, etc., we need to think about how they articulate a specific relationship to class. Such terms may appear to have nothing to do with class, but they constitute it nonetheless, primarily through their reiteration of value on a daily basis' (Skeggs 2004: 44). Having therefore set out some of the key aspects of Skeggs' analysis, in a fairly brisk fashion, I now turn to the most important part of her analysis for my approach, which is the discussion of identity and self.

In broad terms, Skeggs seeks to show how some theories that emphasize the power of a mobile self or the ability to remake the self, tend to lack 'a theory of positioning, a way of understanding how birth into categorizations, known and recognized through inscription, representations, discourse and narrative, but also institutionalized and surveilled, sets limits on the potential for exchange (whether it be through the labour theory of value, renting, asset accrual, or conversion of cultural capital)' (2004: 77). Thus, the mobility of the self is more limited for some people than others. Again, there are many dimensions to this discussion that could be explored, but I focus on the idea that the contemporary self is prosthetic.

Skeggs develops this argument from previous ideas that the self has been aestheticized. Thus, identity, especially for middle-class people, is produced through the expansion of a range of cultural forms engaged with (see further Chapter 8) and through the development of the self as an artistic pursuit through style and so on. Skeggs suggests that such views are based on the idea that self 'accrues' culture, thus having similarities to the view discussed in Chapter 9 of the extended self, produced through enthusiasm. However, as in that discussion, Skeggs argues that the idea of the prosthetic self is different in that it entails play with new forms and ideas (they can be taken on and taken off) and that such theories are 'predicated upon a critique of how certain *perspectives* become legitimated' (p. 137). This idea of prosthetic extension is therefore useful in thinking the idea of the self further.

Skeggs derives this idea from the work of Lury (1998) in particular. The argument is that the:

> [T]rying on, or attachment of and detachment of cultural resources (which she defines as either perceptual or mechanical) makes this

self-extension possible. In adopting/adapting/attaching a prosthesis, the person creates (or is created by) a self-identity that is no longer defined by the edict 'I think therefore I am'; rather, he or she is constituted in the relation 'I can, therefore I am'. Access to resources is therefore central to this 'doing', experimental self.

(Skeggs 2004: 138–9)

Also important is knowledge. Perhaps even more significant is the idea that the extension via the prosthesis involves a performance, which Skeggs develops through the work of Munro (1996) and Strathern (1991, 1992). As I will argue further, with respect to the literature on fandom and enthusiasm in Chapter 9, this is a powerful idea. Skeggs makes the important point that the resources available for this process are unevenly distributed. This is an important point and she also shows how ideas of the self considered in the omnivore thesis (see Chapter 8) imply less playfulness (p. 147).

This discussion has made the important point that these ideas of the self involve connection to a variety of resources and that the working class may be disadvantaged in this. However, while this is no doubt true, I will argue that there are also alternative resources that are available to these groups. This may mean that their selves are extended in different ways. It is here that ideas of the different, not just unequal, resources are important. Moreover, if many of these resources are provided via a media-drenched society, then they are perhaps more widely available than Skeggs suggests.

Another related issue with this idea of the prosthetic self is that, as I have suggested earlier with respect to the work of Bourdieu, it can seem as this is a voluntaristic process, in that people can decide whether or not to engage in such processes. While there will of course be aspects of the process that are like this, it is not a free choice by any means. Despite these points, there is much to be gained via these ideas of the self and I will take them up at several points subsequently. However, I now turn to some related issues of class, culture and morality.

Morality, evaluation and ordinary life

In his book *The Moral Significance of Class*, Sayer (2005) explores a number of important issues in the cultural examination of class. I will not consider all the significant issues that he raises and I do not dwell overly on the theoretical project of his work. In this respect his conjunction of political economy and sociology is both original and thought-provoking. However, it is relatively removed from the specific concerns of my argument. Moreover, I am unable to explore the detail of many of his overall themes. The full discussion of these would take more space than is available here. I therefore seek to draw from his argument some important points that further the approach that I am developing. Thus, in further grounding the aspect of the cultural significance of class in mediatized ordinary life, I mobilize four main aspects of Sayer's argument. First, I rather briefly consider the overall thrust of his argument. Second, I consider aspects of his revision of Bourdieu's idea of the habitus. Third, I extend this examination through the way in which he considers aspects of the dynamics of class in what I have called ordinary life. Fourth, I follow this with consideration of evaluation and responses to the idea and reality of class.

Sayer certainly does not divorce the consideration of cultural aspects of class from structural forces. Indeed he is at pains to link cultural and economic processes. However, I emphasize the way in which he points to the significance of daily and lived experience to the consideration of class. He seeks to explore the moral (which he uses interchangeably with ethical) significance of class, in the area that he calls 'lay normativity' (2005: 2). He sees therefore that ordinary life is infused with and cross-cut by moral and ethical concerns, feelings and rationalities. A significant part of his critique of other theories of class (including the cultural work of Bourdieu) revolves around the way in which they neglect morality and associated issues. This is a version of ordinary life that is characterized as consisting of struggles and competition, but as well where peoples 'strive to flourish' (p. 68). This is all significant to the version of ordinary life here and the approach of Sayer adds some important dimensions to the argument. Furthermore, he also adds some important riders to Bourdieu's concept of the habitus.

Sayer's examination of the idea of the habitus depends on his view of 'the need to develop an understanding of the normative orientation of the habitus, especially its ethical dispositions' (p. 23). Sayer deploys a number of arguments in seven stages to get to his revision of habitus. The outcome of this process is a version of the idea that emphasizes three key aspects: the inter-action of what can be seen as ingrained 'dispositions' and the conscious will to act in diverse ways; the way in which people have space to exercise 'agency' and ordinary reflection on their actions, which enables them to change – what Sayer calls 'mundane reflexivity' (2005: 51); and that people display 'norma-tive orientations, emotions and commitments' (p. 51). Commitments in this formulation are to a range of different aspects of social and cultural life, in ways that recall the work of Karl Mannheim (see Longhurst 1989) on the way in which Marxists characterized the notion of interest in too narrow and econ-omistic a fashion. Thus, Sayer moves even wider than the version of economic, cultural and social versions of interest in Bourdieu. In this context it is important to note that 'people do not strive for resources and recognition, they strive to flourish by living in ways they have reason to value and this depends on more than either resources or recognition' (p. 68).

Sayer develops this approach to consider how people evaluate others in the course of what I have called ordinary life. In general, he identifies three different realms in which such evaluation operates. The first is 'aesthetic: regarding matters such as décor, clothing and personal appearance'. The sec-ond is 'performative: regarding competence and performance, such as that of a doctor or teacher'. The third is 'moral: regarding moral qualities or propriety' (p. 142). Sayer focuses on the moral dimension (although he notes that the three dimensions can overlap). He identifies a number of forms of moral 'sen-timents'. These include 'sympathy or fellow feeling', 'benevolence and gener-osity', 'compassion and pity', 'envy and resentment', 'justice', 'toleration', 'shame' and 'humiliation'. In this discussion, Sayer is careful not simply to emphasize how the exercise of these sentiments can show how human beings have positive feelings for others, but to recognize the downside of class-based interaction as well. This he does through the discussion of shame and humiliation, as well as subsequent consideration of class contempt, which includes 'visceral revulsion, disgust and sneering, through the tendency not to see or hear others as people, to the subtlest forms of aversion' (p. 163). However, he does note that it is important that sociology should not neglect the positive aspects of these moral sentiments. This is an important way of characterizing the modes of moral interaction in ordinary life in its complexity and shows an important development of the overall approach of Bourdieu.

This approach is extended in Sayer's consideration of different responses to class. He recognizes, as has been discussed earlier, that the ways in which people 'act towards class others involve varying mixes of pursuit of advantage, deference, resistance and pursuit of goods for their own sake. But they are also influenced by their moral sentiments and norms, which are only partially inflected according to class and other social divisions' (p. 169). However, even the positive aspects of this are contextualized by 'the field of class forces in ways that reproduce class hierarchy' (p. 169). Sayer considers four responses to class: 'egalitarian tendencies, the pursuit of respect and respectability, class pride and moral boundary drawing' (p. 169). All these responses are affected by the structural nature of class itself. Sayer also suggests that these responses take place in the context of wider understandings of 'their own and others' behaviour and to their views of class itself' (p. 186).

It is important through this brief consideration of the work of Sayer to note how discursive interaction around the complexities of class runs through ordinary life and I have introduced his work to make this point and to show one of the important ways in which this area can be researched.

Conclusion

In this chapter, I have explored a number of different dimensions of a new class and culture agenda. As I stated in the introduction, this is important for my argument in several ways. Here I wish to emphasize both the continuing significance of class in structural terms, but also the way in which class is a significant part of the interactions and performances of ordinary life and identity. I have spent time on the general approach and two specific studies to pull out the different ways in which class is currently being theorized and researched in a broad context of culture. This both shows the significance of class but also that it can be seen in the context of the aims of this book. I will pick up some further aspects of this case in the chapters that follow. For the moment, it is important to emphasize that I see this work on class as significant in a number of ways. First, it has opened up new avenues of the consideration of class that emphasize the cultural. This means that it has the potential to close the gap between sociology and media/cultural studies. Second, this work shows how a dimension of mediatized ordinary life can be considered to illuminate particular key aspects (there are, of course, others). Third, this approach has developed the theorization of the individual, identity and the self in ways that can be further developed by more explicit consideration of the media (see further Chapter 9). I now turn to the related processes of distinguishing.

7   Distinguishing *and* connecting 1: capitals *and the* use *of* time

One of the key arguments of this book is that a full understanding of the nature of ordinary life requires attention to a range of different types of evidence. In particular I seek to integrate ideas, theories and research from sociology, cultural and media studies. In the previous chapter, I explored the implications of such an approach for the study and theorization of contemporary identities, in particular those around class. This chapter continues that approach but takes the argument in a different direction. In broad terms, it is the first of three chapters that can be seen as exploring how people use their time in contemporary advanced capitalist societies to consider how it is that belonging, distinguishing and individualizing are performed and audienced. In particular, the focus of this chapter is on some arguments concerning the use of time and how this relates to different modes of capital. These were introduced in an earlier chapter, where Bourdieu and Putnam's arguments were briefly considered. In different ways, these chapters have a focus on the way in which time is used, especially in relation to how time and activity might be described as social capital. Chapter 8 discusses in some detail the debates on the omnivore thesis, which has been an influential argument about the way in which the activities that people engage in are changing has implications for the nature of the bonds between people and how they distinguish themselves from others. Chapter 9 treats some of the more recent literature on fandom and celebrity in a similar fashion. It is an important part of my argument, that research in each of these fields has tended to be relatively isolated from that in the other two, even though they are often addressing what are actually quite similar issues. These are to do with how time is spent, what are its implications for the nature of the relationships between people, how people see themselves as different from others, and so on.

In this chapter, I explore three themes that I see as offering some light on the way in which people seek to reproduce forms of advantage through their activities. First, this will mean exploring some of the more sociological evidence on how people use their time. Therefore, I begin with a fairly brisk summary of the long-run trends in this. This I suggest provides a context for the more specific consideration of modes of distinction in the rest of the chapter. Second, this is followed by consideration of some of the evidence

more specifically about the distribution and changing nature of social capital
in Britain, drawing to some extent on the data in the British Household Panel
Survey. Third, I explore some of the more complex dynamics in the relationships between economic, cultural and social capital in the reproduction of
advantage in schooling, drawing on the work of Devine (2004) in particular. It
is important to emphasize that other areas of research could have been considered for analysis in this chapter, but that those that are discussed show the
significance of social and cultural change and allow further building blocks to
be erected in the argument concerning how people belong and distinguish
themselves is societies that are increasingly centred around performing and
audiencing.

Time use

There is distinctive and specialist attention to the use of time in contemporary
societies and over a long-run period that is informed by a number of disciplines. I will not enter into this extensive literature in any depth, as my point is
to consider some of the most significant issues that it raises and what might be
seen as the state of the art of findings about how we use our time. A very
helpful discussion of these areas can be found in the work of Gershuny (2000). I
will only address some key aspects of this book, as they help me move forward
the general arguments that I am making.

Gershuny argues that there are three main trends or what he calls convergences in the use of time in industrial/postindustrial societies, based on an
extensive review of the literature. These trends provide an overall picture of
how time is deployed within and across societies. Gershuny explores the relationship between the use of time across three activities: paid work, unpaid
work and leisure/consumption. He says that there is fourth category – sleep –
but that this can be seen as residual as it is activity which 'for any social group,
to within very few minutes per day [is] a constant over historical time' (p. 5).
The three convergences are with respect national, gender and status groups.

First, nations are over time becoming more alike in the balance between
paid and unpaid work:

> We find over the developed countries in the latter half of the twenti-
> eth century there appears to be an approximately constant balance
> between the totals of paid and unpaid work in a society (generally
> around 55 per cent paid, 45 per cent). The twenty countries we shall be
> discussing in this book show overall a general increase in leisure (i.e. a
> decline in the total of paid plus unpaid work), though some of the richer
> countries, towards the end of the century, show a small decline in leisure
> time.
>
> (Gershuny 2000: 5)

Second, he points to a process of gender difference and convergence for
all the countries for which the evidence is reviewed:

> Women in each country, and throughout the period, do on average
> much more domestic work and much less paid work, than men, and the

> majority of men's work is certainly paid work . . . And generally the total
> balances of work versus leisure, for men and women, in any country at
> any point in history, are approximately the same. But over time the
> balances change. The women come to do absolutely more paid, and
> absolutely less unpaid work. The men do generally less paid and increase
> their unpaid. So the trends for the sexes, are clearly convergent.
>
> (Gershuny 2000: 5–6)

Finally, there is a convergence with respect to status, but with a more complex
set of processes behind it that interact to produce the trend. To summarize the
position:

> There is thus overall convergence in time use between the groups, with
> more leisure time overall. But an alternative summary of the changes
> is: *a reversal of the previous status–leisure gradient.* Those of higher status
> previously had more leisure, and subsequently had less of it, than those
> of lower social status.
>
> (Gershuny 2000: 7)

These are significant trends as a broad picture of what is going on in the
patterns of time use in ordinary life. However, there are other important features to which Gershuny draws our attention. The first of these is the significance of the micro-differences in modern ordinary life. Thus, as he points out
while there are long-run trends and convergences, there may be specific differences and some of the specific differences around consumption practices are
potentially important for the overall argument of this book. Thus, if the time
available for different forms of consumption is increasing, as the proportion of
time spent on work decreases, then arguments about how that leisure time is
spent become of increased social and cultural significance. As Gershuny says
there are 'multiple cross-cutting cleavages in leisure' (p. 32). This he suggests
can, in one sense, be seen as support for some postmodernist arguments: 'what
we find is to some extent consistent with writings of the "post-modernist"
school: diversifications of consumption styles, the absence of a "leading social
class" ' (p. 42) (see also the discussion of postmodernism and the omnivore
thesis in Chapter 8). Gershuny distinguishes his argument from that of the
postmodernists, as he wishes to retain an emphasis on 'modernization as a
continuing theme in developed societies' (p. 42). This is a point that I agree
with and I have used the work of Lipovetsky and ideas of hypermodernization
earlier in the book to offer some measure of theorization of the processes
involved. Thus, we have an argument that places some degree of emphasis
on leisure and consumption, and, even more importantly, that the modes
of differentiation that occur in this sphere are of some social and cultural
significance.

A second key theme to which Gershuny draws our attention is the relationship between the detailed use of time across the days of ordinary life, the
processes of the life course and the long-run processes. Thus, we can consider
patterns of time use across the day and this will enable us to consider the
'significance of the mundane' (Gershuny 2000: 18) in ways that chime with my
emphases on the detail of the processes of ordinary life. Thus, for example, we

can research the ways in which individuals structure their days and the patterns of a typical week. These are often very informative ways of identifying patterns of activity that might not be found if people are simply asked about one mode of activity in isolation. As we found in the research that informs *Globalization and Belonging* (Savage et al. 2005), when asked about the pattern of a week and a typical weekend, activities and memberships of groups are sometimes brought to mind in interviewees when perhaps they had been overlooked. However, it is important that these activities on daily and weekly cycles are related to stages in lifecycles or to the life course. Berthoud and Gershuny (2000: 230–1) in their discussion of the British Household Panel Survey (BHPS; see later), distinguish between eight different life stages for individuals:

- dependent child
- young adult
- unattached
- young family
- older family
- older childless
- retired
- old/infirm.

As Berthoud and Gershuny (2000: 231) suggest: 'This categorisation is intended as a genuine sequence', although, of course, some people will miss stages. Thus, the patterns of time use through a day, week or year, can be connected to the particular life stage that people are living at that point. For example, those with young children are more likely to engage in some activities compared with those without and so on. This matters to the way that people use their time and to their experience of a range of activities. As will be discussed later in the chapter, it has impacts on the way in which people seek to help their children to progress through the education system. It also has implications for the way in which people connect to the media.

The BHPS is, as its name suggests, a panel study where broadly the same people are revisited with similar questions at regular intervals. This is a very powerful instrument for tracking social and cultural changes. A similar exercise has been performed for television viewing by the British Film Institute (BFI) tracking study. The results of this are summarized by Gauntlett and Hill (1999). The research that this book reports on had its beginnings in a 1988 study where 22,000 people wrote a diary about their television viewing on 1 November 1988. On the basis of this study, the BFI tracking study was initiated, which studied a sample of people who 'self-selected' from the earlier research. The sample was 'generally' representative of the UK population. At the beginning of the study there were 509 respondents and at the conclusion, there were 427. Between 1991 and 1996 the respondents completed 15 questionnaire diaries. The study produced a number of significant findings, especially for the arguments being advanced here.

Drawing on the key findings that are summarized in the book, it is possible to pull out important points with respect to: television and everyday life; news consumption; transitions and change; personal meanings; video and technology in the home; the retired and elderly; gender; and television violence. I will briefly consider these findings with the aim of building up the picture of the patterns of ordinary life, which is a key aim of this chapter.

With respect to everyday life, or as I have preferred to name it ordinary life, the diaries analysed by Gauntlett and Hill show that there is an organized schedule or pattern to everyday life and that TV programmes can provide important markers to the day. However, the schedule is not fixed and it can vary by, for example day, week and season. While some people planned their viewing in detail and others did not, all had awareness of what was being shown on television. Television acted as a focal point for households and because of this it could be a locus of dispute within the household. A final important point that emerged was that hobbies or what can best be termed enthusiasms were important for a number of people, especially those who communicated that they had the spare time to enjoy them.

Gauntlett and Hill (1999) specifically report on the consumption of news by the diarists. While this is less important for my overall argument than some of the more general points concerning everyday life, it is resonant because of the general argument that Putnam (2000) makes about the effect of TV viewing on social capital and the points made by Norris (2000) in return that it surely matters what and how people watch. Thus, if people are engaging with news this could potentially be helpful for knowledge of current affairs and so on. Thus, Gauntlett and Hill found that watching the news was a social activity and that like other aspects of TV viewing, it related to the patterns of everyday life and was affected by life course changes, and so on. Importantly, men and women both stated that they liked to watch the news, although women were more constrained by time.

The importance of the life course was brought out by their data on life transitions. Young adults were aware of TV's role at transitional points in life, and major life transitions (such as marriage, divorce and having children) affected TV viewing to a significant extent. Adults were more likely to have established patterns of viewing than younger people and TV could be used in specific ways at times of emotional crisis (Gauntlett and Hill 1999: 103):

> For some respondents, television is a distraction, or an opportunity to avoid confrontation. For others, television is a means to build up strength, in a similar way that one might build up one's energy after an illness. This is admitted, in general terms, by this respondent:
>
>> During major emotional crises (i.e. bereavement, separation) I find I watch a lot more TV, for hours at a time. When you have no emotional energy left it's very easy to watch anything. As my energy returns I become more selective in my viewing again.
>>
>> (33 year old female office manager)

Television also had a variety of different meanings to people. For some it offers companionship and can act a 'friend' to them. People were sometimes 'guilty' about their TV viewing and this was especially the case with the watching of TV during the daytime. Talk about television was a part of many people's lives and television had a role in people's identities but even within a detailed study such as this, this was difficult to pin down.

With respect to more interactive TV technologies, video-recording machines were regularly used and time shifting of programmes played a role in the development of routines that were structured by the respondents rather than being determined by the scheduling decisions of the television companies. A range of uses had developed, for example, 'by cutting too-long programmes into handy chunks, for "caching" information which they needed, for storing video "cuttings" on items of importance to them, for establishing international friendships, and for shifting and checking material to protect children' (Gauntlett and Hill 1999: 171). Some people had developed video collections and these tended to be 'cult TV' for younger people and 'quality' TV for older people. Most people were optimistic about the future development of television technologies, though there were concerns about new technologies in terms of 'cost, aesthetics and available time' (p. 171).

One of the many strengths of the research that Gauntlett and Hill report on was that it produced some detailed findings on the retired and elderly – a group of relatively heavy television viewers. It is important to recognize, as Gauntlett and Hill do, that this is a diverse group and that there are a range of different responses to retirement. Some older people reported to being self-conscious about watching TV, and this 'stems partly from having grown up in a world where television was not part of everyday life' (p. 207). As people get older they tend to spend more time with TV and this may be caused by financial and physical restrictions, but older people also thought that TV enabled them to keep in touch with the world. Their tastes varied but they tended to prefer 'gentle' and 'pleasant' TV.

Gauntlett and Hill illuminate some significant findings with respect to gender and TV. In so doing they comment on some earlier influential research on this topic. Particularly important in this respect has been the work of Morley (1986). They report that many people rejected the idea that men and women have different tastes in TV programmes. Moreover, that many men reported their enjoyment of soap operas on TV. This goes against much conventional academic and lay wisdom. Some women felt that the range of women represented on TV should be extended. A minority of respondents objected to the depiction of gay and lesbian lifestyles and this was combined in some cases with expressions of racism. In households with at least one adult man and woman, decisions about what to watch are made, in the main, jointly, although in a small minority of cases men made such decisions. In these households with a male and female adult the man normally retained possession of the remote control for the television, but this did not mean that he actually controlled the viewing.

Dealing with one of the 'classic' debates with respect to TV viewing, Gauntlett and Hill address the vexed issue of violence on TV (see also, for an excellent 'debunking' of a number of conventional arguments, Barker and Brooks 1998). They show that viewers distinguish between fictional and factual violence and that they are more concerned about fictional violence than other forms of material that are often seen as controversial. Respondents believe that children should be protected and they are in favour of the television watershed, which prevents the screening of such material before 9 pm in the evening. However, there was disagreement among respondents about what acceptable levels of violence were and views on this issue do change over time.

Gauntlett and Hill identify some overall conclusions to their research, which are of significance for my argument here. First, they make points about time. People scheduled their viewing and were concerned about the time that they spent watching TV. Moreover:

> Time was also a factor in broader terms, as over the five years in which the participants wrote diaries we were able to observe the significance of transitions, changes and shifts in the character of their lives. Starting or finishing a relationship, periods of depression or grief, or changes in a person's perception of how generally 'busy' they were (for example, if exams were imminent, or had just passed), as well as the changing attention requirements of other members of a household or family, could all have an effect upon how much TV was watched, and the quality of engagement with it.
>
> (Gauntlett and Hill 2005: 284)

Second, there were some particularly important findings with respect to gender. Specifically, they say that 'we generally found some breakdown of the polarised distinction between men's and women's tastes and the uses of the media that previous studies had emphasised'. Some specific findings with respect to these issues have already been summarized earlier. They suggest that these studies should be seen as more 'of their time' than they are often seen to be.

Third, as has been summarized earlier, the relationship between television and identity was fine grained:

> People's individual identities are clearly touched by the media in very gentle ways: whilst the ways in which people see themselves and others may be subtly influenced by many different television elements, this is not something which we would be able to trace in a study of this kind.
>
> (Gauntlett and Hill 2005: 287)

This is perhaps a more significant finding than Gauntlett and Hill recognize, as it does suggest that very generalizing arguments about media and identity change should be treated with some degree of caution, in favour of the recognition of the complexities involved that are shown by empirical research.

Fourth, they conclude that television is seen as 'seductive' by respondents. People seek to resist TV. As we found (Savage et al. 2005), people are defensive about their television watching. They want to say that they do not watch it or that they only watch particular types of programme (see, further, Chapter 8). People seek to structure their viewing. Some control over TV overload was maintained by the way in which programming seemed to be divided into three types: *favourite* programmes, which were always watched, or else would ideally be taped; other programmes, which would be *routinely* watched but which would not be listed as favourites – the news and teatime soaps were particularly likely to be in this category; and other shows, which would be watched because they happened to be on, looked engaging enough and there was time to see them (p. 288).

Finally, they offer some comments on the idea of fragmentation. As Gauntlett and Hill suggest: 'The idea of the "fragmented audience" has been a popular way of considering changes in the reception of television, following from the changing face of broadcasting for some time now. But we found little evidence of it' (p. 288). In addition:

> It is worth noting from this study not only the particular point that British audiences refused to fragment much in the first half of the 1990s, but the more general and important finding that people's social impulses will most likely mean that they will not become fragmented, isolated viewers to the extent that some have predicted.
>
> (Gauntlett and Hill 2005: 288–9)

This is important as going against some of the excessive claims for fragmentation of more extreme postmodernist writers. However, it does show both the significance of TV and its patterned consumption (see also Savage et al. 2005). Moreover, this very important study has shown how television is related to a number of other important features of social and cultural life. In addition, it points to how difficult it is to study the subtleties of identity even through such long-term research. The way of thinking about such issues involves the development, I argue, of the sort of approach represented by this book. It also captures the detail of how people use time with particular attention to TV.

This fairly brief consideration of time use in general and with specific attention to TV has drawn attention to three related processes of time use that are of significance for the argument here. First, there is the everyday micro-time use that can be studied usually on the basis of some kind of diary or through interviews, that looks at the rhythms of the day, week and year (rhythms that are reflected and constructed by media schedulers, although what is broadcast at what time and on what day of the week; as well as through the significance of fixed sporting events like World Cups and so on). Second, there are the changes that take place across the life course and the fact that people pass through different life stages. Third, there is the way in which these processes come together to produce the long-run trends, which this section began by considering. These processes need to be more directly combined with other forms of evidence about what is happening to the processes of ordinary life.

Social capital in Britain

In Chapter 3, I introduced some of the work on social capital, especially that associated with Putnam (2000). There I also stated that his work had led to much debate about the theorization of social capital and its effects. As this debate progressed, Putnam and Goss (2002: 9–10) argued that four important distinctions had emerged with respect to social capital: 'formal versus informal', 'thick versus thin', 'inward-looking versus outward-looking' and 'bridging versus bonding'. These are useful and in the main fairly straightforward distinctions. Formal versus informal captures the distinction between an organized group and a loose grouping that may have some social rules, but does not have officers, and so on. Thick versus thin summarizes the difference between being with the same group of people over a range of activities:

> Some forms of social capital are closely interwoven and multistranded, such as a group of steelworkers who work together every day at the factory, go out for drinks on Saturday, and go to mass every Sunday. There are also very thin, almost invisible filaments of social capital, such as the nodding acquaintance you have with the person you occasionally see waiting in line at the supermarket, or even a chance encounter with another person in an elevator.
>
> (Putnam and Goss 2002: 10)

Inward-looking versus outward-looking shows that 'Some forms of social capital are, by choice or necessity, inward-looking and tend to promote the material, social, or political interests of their own members, while others are outward-looking and concern themselves with public goods' (Putnam and Goss 2002: 11). Finally, there is the related distinction between bridging and bonding, which has already been introduced in Chapter 3. To recap: 'Bonding social capital brings together people who are like one another in important respects (ethnicity, age, gender, social class, and so on), whereas bridging social capital refers to social networks that bring people together who are unlike one another' (Putnam and Goss 2002: 11). One important aspect of the debate around Putnam's work involved consideration of the extent to which the thesis of the decline in social capital and trust applied to other comparable societies. The work of Hall (2002) considered these issues in some depth and it is important to our deeper understanding of the nature of ordinary life in the UK.

Hall considers trends in social capital in five areas: 'membership in voluntary associations'; 'charitable endeavour'; 'informal sociability'; 'generation effects'; and 'social trust'. He shows that there has not been a decline in the membership of voluntary associations, indeed:

> [O]verall levels of associational membership in Britain seem to have been at least as high in the 1980s and 1990s as they were in 1959, and perhaps somewhat higher. Even when the respondents' levels of education are held constant, the basic inclination of the vast majority of the British populace to join associations remained roughly the same in 1990 as it was in the 1950s.
>
> (Hall 2002: 25)

The same holds good for charitable work. Likewise the data on informal sociability, as derived from the sort of research discussed in the previous section, seem to suggest that if anything there has been a rise in this. Hall argues, for example, that increased television viewing has substituted for radio listening. TV viewing in this argument does not lead to decline in other activities (although as this book suggests it may change the *nature* of them). Hall adds the caveat that the change in habits may have already have happened by the time that the data are considered, that is, the beginning of the 1950s. Moreover, Hall argues that there are not the generational effects in Britain that Putnam found in the USA. Finally, despite the rise (or at least stability) in indicators of social capital, social trust has fallen in Britain. This is potentially significant. As Hall says:

> First, overall levels of social trust declined between 1959, when 56 percent of respondents said they generally trusted others, and 1990, when only 44 percent said they did. There is almost certainly a period effect here of some magnitude. Second, the erosion in social trust has been more sub-stantial among some groups than others . . . the decline in social trust has been greater among the working class than the middle class.
>
> (Hall 2002: 32–3)

Moreover, there are significant differences between age cohorts with younger groups being less trusting.

Hall argues that three factors cause this stability 'and perhaps even growth in community involvement in Britain over the years' (p. 34). These are first, 'a radical transformation in the education system, marked by a massive expansion of both secondary and postsecondary education'; second, 'a change in the overall class structure of British society, driven by economic and politi-cal developments, which have altered the distribution of occupations and life situations across the populace'; and, third, 'characteristically British forms of government action that have done much to encourage and sustain voluntary community involvement' (2002: 35). In general, the higher the levels of edu-cational attainment, the higher the levels of social capital. As British society has become better educated then the consequent rise in social capital can com-pensate for falls that otherwise might have occurred. Moreover, participation by women has increased greatly:

> Social capital has been sustained in Britain largely by virtue of the increas-ing participation of women in the community. This effect might result from any of three long term developments: the increased exposure of women to higher education; the growing participation of women in the labor force; or more general changes in the attitudes and social situation of women, partly under the influence of the feminist movement.
>
> (Hall 2002: 37)

The second factor concerns significant effects of changes in the class structure. In summary, the middle classes have more communal interactions and a greater involvement in voluntary associations and the class structure has shifted so that there are more middle-class occupations. This should have a positive effect on levels of social capital. Third, government has worked along-side the voluntary sector in Britain and therefore has sponsored its continuing development.

One significant point has already been introduced concerning the decline in social trust. Hall suggests that it is difficult to be definitive about what might be causing this, although it might be that, for example, the sorts of association that people are involved with lessens trust rather than generates it. Political trust can also be seen to have declined in Britain. However, this does not mean that political participation has suffered accordingly: 'Levels of political participation remain high in Britain despite low levels of trust in politicians and political institutions' (p. 52). A key issue that remains, however, is the distribution of social capital across the population. This is particularly the case in class terms, but is also true with respect to age. Thus, Hall argues that: 'The two groups who face marginalization from civil society are the working class and the young' (p. 53). This could have significant future effects (see later) if such trends continue.

Hall's work is therefore important in illustrating some key aspects of social life in contemporary Britain, pointing to the continued importance of associative life in Britain. However, it also shows that trust is in decline and that social factors concerning education, class and the actions of government have sustained this picture. Moreover, the divisions between those who have social capital and those who do not and those who trust and those who do not may be getting worse.

Hall's work is useful on a number of levels for the argument of this book. He points to the continued salience and significance of social capital in Britain, illuminates its key contours and introduces a number of arguments concerning the explanation for these processes. Furthermore, in particular, he offers evidence for the complex relationship of media consumption to other dimensions of social capital. However, it is also important to consider whether these processes have been subject to further change in recent years. Thus with respect to the media it can be suggested that recent changes, contextualized by political processes of deregulation and technological/economic ones of media convergence around digitization may be producing an environment, where media will have a different relation to social capital processes. However, before this argument can be further considered in the rest of this book, it is necessary to update the trends that Hall identified.

This has been done in some collaborative work on political engagement (Warde et al. 2003). We used the BHPS to update the work done by Hall on political engagement. As with the work on TV discussed earlier, the BHPS is a very useful survey as it tracks a sample that 'was designed to remain broadly representative of the population of Great Britain as it changed through the 1990s' (Warde et al. 2003: 515). It was:

> Designed as a annual survey of each adult (16+) member of a nationally representative sample of more than 5,000 households, making a total of approximately 10,000 individual interviewees. The same individuals were re-interviewed in successive waves and, if some had already separated from their original households, all adult members of their new households were also interviewed. Children were interviewed once they reached the age of 16: there was also a special survey of 11–15 year old household members from Wave 4 onwards.
>
> (Warde et al. 2003: 515)

We examined membership and political activism through the 1990s using these data. Four key points emerged. First, the characterization of Hall, that Britain is not suffering a decline in social capital as demonstrated by Putnam for the USA, was confirmed. As measured by memberships of voluntary associations, social capital has held steady during the 1990s and might even have increased. Second, there is also a continued increase in female participation. Third, again in agreement with Hall, we found that there was increased polarisation in the class base of social capital. The difference is increasingly between the service class and the rest. Fourth, and perhaps most significantly, we drew an important finding from the panel aspect of the BHPS. Thus, there is some volatility in voluntary association membership. Therefore:

> In the light of the large numbers of people who move in and out of organizations from year to year, Britain appears to be a more participatory and active society that might otherwise be imagined. Very few people were never members of any association in the 1990s, a mere 15.6 per cent. Most associations, including political parties and social movements, had people move in and out of membership at a substantial and steady rate.
>
> (Warde et al. 2003: 525)

This finding can be interpreted positively in that it shows that people are more engaged than a snapshot approach might suggest and that they are gaining associational benefits from meeting other people. However, it might also suggest that people are actually not that committed to their memberships.

These approaches to social capital, based in quantitative data, and with particular attention to impact on politics and levels of trust, facilitate the construction of a picture of the state of these aspects of ordinary life in contemporary Britain. In short, we are still involved and engaged, the engagement of women has increased, but the class differences in engagement are increasingly salient. This might be even more worrying given the way in which Gershuny shows that it is the middle classes that are feeling more harried and that their time for social engagement is potentially under threat. However, despite the continued significance of social engagement, we are becoming less socially and politically trusting. This might be attributed to the 'debunking' role that is played by media, in that there are increased numbers of programmes that question the activities of politicians (through the 24-hour news culture) and of a range of professional groups from plumbers to doctors (through exposure to reality TV and contemporary drama). These can only be speculations at this point. However, they do introduce two key issues with the sorts of data discussed in this chapter so far. First, the relationship between social capital and other activities (apart from politics in the broadest sense) requires consideration. For example, it would be useful to explore the impact of these processes in social capital on cultural capital in more depth. Second, it is important to get behind the quantitative data to explore how these processes are happening and what they mean to people. I now move on to consider these issues.

Class and education: economic, cultural and social resources

There are a number of ways in which the relationship between economic, cultural and social capitals can be explored; however, I will focus on one recent study that has considered these relationships through qualitative data in a detailed discussion of education and the middle class.

In *Class Practices: How Parents Help Their Children Get Good Jobs*, Devine (2004) reports on an interview study with middle-class people in the USA and the UK. She considers the experiences of interviewees as children and younger people (i.e. how their parents sought to help them in their educational progress) and as parents (i.e. what they are doing to help their own children progress). Devine's analysis is partly an outcrop from the tradition of British class theory, but as with the literature considered in the previous chapter, I consider that it is pertinent outside some of the sometimes sectarian and increasing technicist parameters of some aspects of that activity. It also represents another aspect of the approach that seeks to connect class back to a range of cultural activities.

Devine voices her dissatisfaction with the more narrow economically based versions of class analysis, some of which are informed by rational action theory (RAT). In particular, she admires the focus of writers such as John Goldthorpe on resources that are used as a base for class advancement, but suggests that he conceives them in too narrow and economistic ways. In many respects she argues, his analysis is close to that of Bourdieu, which, as shown in an earlier chapter, does consider a range of resources theorized in different forms of capital. Devine seeks to reintegrate the different forms of capital in analysis of class advancement, without making narrow assumptions about the reasons for human action:

> While I have always believed in the importance of human agency, that people make choices and make decisions, I have never liked the economistic and often brutal sounding nature of cost-benefit analysis. Social life – especially family life – has always seemed much richer than that to me. In sum, it was my view that much has been lost in the explicit development of a theory of middle-class reproduction.
>
> (Devine 2004: 7)

Having carried out lengthy qualitative interviews in the UK and the USA, Devine finds that the parents of her interviewees did indeed seek to mobilize, and in many cases did succeed in mobilizing, economic resources on their behalf. Thus, in the USA parents 'used their money indirectly in being able to afford to live in affluent communities where they could send their children to good public schools'; whereas 'in Britain, economic resources were used directly and indirectly to ensure children secured entry into the best state grammar schools possible' (p. 175). Those from more modest backgrounds who have succeeded did so via the better parts of the state sector and with as much financial help as their parents could provide. Thus the nature of the education system in the 1950s, 1960s and 1970s was of help to those seeking to advance themselves. The changing nature of that system had introduced greater uncertainty for the interviewees in promoting the advancement of their own children. This meant that economic resources had increased in importance. Sometimes this meant that education was paid for privately. This was, of course, more difficult for the less affluent: 'Middle-class reproduction, for these parents, therefore, was not easy or straightforward especially when the mobilisation of economic resources could only increase the propensity for academic success, but certainly could not guarantee it' (p. 177). This meant that some of the children had had difficult educational paths and had not been successful in conventional terms. Thus, in these processes where successful, there had been a conversion of economic resources (capital) into cultural ones. Further, that these cultural resources are connected to social ones.

Cultural resources had also been used on behalf of the interviewees and they were seeking to use them for their own children. However, an important issue is how those who come from backgrounds that are relatively modest in terms of cultural capital have managed to succeed. In this respect, Devine suggests that this shows some drawbacks with Bourdieu's theories, however, 'there is considerable merit to Bourdieu's ideas, for he captures the different ways in which those in modest positions engage with the education system' (p. 180). Again, Devine places an important emphasis on the uncertainties of these situations. Investment of capital does not always ensure success. Cultural resources are important, especially in the extent to which parents have knowledge of the education system and are able to guide their children appropriately.

With respect to social resources or social capital, Devine argues that these both tend to slip out of the analyses of Goldthorpe and Bourdieu (p. 182). She found that social capital was important in both the UK and the USA. 'Overall, therefore, the privileged parents of my interviewees certainly drew on their social networks, both intentionally and unintentionally, in helping their children do well' (p. 183). However, the less well off had also used social contacts to their benefit. Likewise, the interviewees were seeking 'to shape their children's own emerging social networks to enhance the chances of educational success' (p. 184). Again there are uncertainties, as nothing will guarantee success.

Devine emphasizes the interconnections of the forms of capital that she has studied in this case:

> [S]ocial resources are as important as economic and cultural resources in the pursuit of educational and occupational success. That said, like cultural resources, social resources are inclusive rather than exclusive goods in that people have more or less of them rather than all or none of them.
>
> (Devine 2004: 185)

This relativity is important, as it shows that forms of capital can be mobilized in specific contexts even if some people will have more or less of them. There are important lessons for public policy that Devine draws from her research in particular concerning the role of access to the education system in as equal a way as possible in promoting social mobility and equality in advanced capitalist countries such as the UK and the USA.

The particular significance of Devine's study for my approach to ordinary life is threefold. First, as argued in the previous chapter, attention to ordinary life does not mean that issues such as class become less important to analysis. Actually the opposite is the case. However, this does entail retheorization of what class actually means, especially if it requires casting the analysis wider than economic logics and occupational classifications. Second, and related, is the fact that economic, cultural and social resources intertwine in processes of inequality and distinction. Devine shows very well and in some detail (which I have not discussed) how this happens. Analysis of none of these capitals of their own is sufficient to the overall analysis. Third, she shows how the consideration of these issues requires attention to the way in which people pursue their own actions, even if these are not theorized via RAT. Moreover, these actions are shown to have a significant measure of contingency about them. In part, such contingency might be explained by the changing structural or institutional context, especially in this case with respect to the education system. However, while this may be important as context, it is not a sufficient explanation on its own.

Conclusion

In this chapter, I have summarized and outlined some important research on different dimensions of ordinary life. The specific areas investigated include political and voluntary participation, TV viewing and schooling. There are four levels on which I wish to conclude this discussion emphasizing long-run trends, the life course/life stages, the organization of the year, month, week and day, and that human social action remains of significance in all these processes.

First, I have used the work discussed to point to long-run trends and convergences in time use and social capital. These discussions are important as they illuminate how what has been happening over a significant period, but also mean that we can consider some over-hyped arguments for the pace of change with some degree of scepticism. However, within such a context, which might point to more stability in social and cultural life than some commentators have suggested, it is then important to recognize the shifts that are taking place, such as the increased perception of pressure on middle-class lifestyles, the polarization in the distribution of social capital and associational membership, the importance of more subtle cultural distinctions, and so on. Thus, there is a situation where these significant changes can be related to longer-run processes. Likewise, there can be seen to be long-run processes in how people seek to act to benefit their children with respect to education. Again, however, significant contemporary changes can be seen, especially related to institutional changes in education itself. Change is not happening overnight, but it is happening.

Second, I have drawn out arguments that show that the stage of life that a person is at is culturally significant. This may seem obvious, but it is surprising how much the point has actually been neglected as cultural experience has been related to social cleavages such as class and gender. While the idea of life stage and life course is part of discussions that consider how culture or specific parts of it relates to youth culture (e.g. Laughey 2006), generation (see 'classically' Mannheim 1952), or to older age and so on, my emphasis here has been slightly different in that I have sought to show the process nature of the life stages. This is significant, I feel, in seeking to capture the trajectory of cultural consumption through different life stages, which will be affected by structural constraints but will also show some commonality with tastes from a previous stage on the part of the individual. The interaction between these different dimensions is of some significance.

Third, I have pointed to the importance of the micro-processes of the ordering of time and activity over the year, month, week, day, and so on.

Discussions of TV are very useful for showing how forms of media consumption allow the ordering of ordinary life. It is important to emphasize that such ordering does not mean that people write a plan of how they are going to live their life or spend their time. As Gauntlett and Hill (1999) show to good effect, such planning is often informal and implicit. These cycles to everyday life are therefore significant, but also in common with the arguments that I have mounted during the course of this book so far, becoming more spectacular and performed. Thus, the events that punctuate and mark these cycles are becoming increasingly salient. As I was writing this in May 2006, the supermarkets where I live were full of accessories to mark England's participation in the football World Cup and many cars were displaying the Flag of St George a full month before the tournament began. Events like this may not happen every day, but they do show how the rhythms are being increasingly marked and marketed.

Finally, it is important to recognize that there is human agency involved in this situation. People are taking active decisions to display particular flags, to join or to remove themselves from voluntary associations, to watch particular programmes on TV and about how best to seek to advance their children's education. All these processes can be seen as aspects of the idea of elective belonging that I have discussed at various points of the book so far. At this point, it is the elective aspect that requires emphasis. I can elect whether or not to display the flag and so on. However, it is also to reiterate the perhaps rather obvious point that there will be other outcomes to these processes than my action intended. This is well captured by Devine's discussion of education. Thus, while parents may make every effort to advance their children's education, this is still subject to a significant degree of uncertainty. Investments are not always successful. The integration of this level of analysis with the others is of great importance.

It is important that these common sorts of conclusion can be drawn from work, which on the face of it has very different theoretical contexts and different specific objects of analysis. Thus, the different backgrounds discussed include economics, political science, sociological considerations of class and media studies. Moreover, specific research topics range from TV to voluntary associational membership to education. These analyses can be integrated into an account of ordinary life. Moreover, it also shows, as argued at the start of this book that ideas about time use, different forms of capital and agency can be related to significant effect. Moreover, it is important to recognize that the chapter has also shown by implication how these processes are involved in distinction. Thus people will want to show that they are not like all the others who watch too much TV. Moreover, seeking to advance the education of your children could involve them in doing better than others. While I have sought on a number of levels to detail the evidence in this chapter, it is important to recognize the overall significance of these particular processes in the context where these processes are increasingly performed for other social audiences.

8 Distinguishing *and* connecting 2: *the* omnivore thesis

Earlier in this book, I suggested that a key process to be examined in the consideration of cultural change is fragmentation. My suggestion was that this idea had, in many respects, in an earlier stage of debate on cultural change, been wrapped up in the idea of postmodernism. While I certainly do not advocate a return to this idea, there is a danger that the ideas that it sought to examine and social and cultural processes considered under its head gain less attention that they should, given its demise (Matthewman and Hoey 2006). I have therefore examined some of the claims around hypermodernity in this 'conceptual space' and have tried to follow through on some of the processes that I think are important in this space in the earlier parts of this book.

As I also argued earlier, one of the big problems with the debate on postmodernism, especially in sociology and in the more social and cultural forms of cultural and media studies, was that it was based on rather little substantive empirical evidence. Some of the reasons for this are obvious. On one level, the theory was meant to be a prompt to research and it might not have been expected that there would be detailed empirical work to back it up. It might have been expected that such research would follow along subsequently. This after all is the nature of 'normal science'. However, more importantly, the philosophical and theoretical stance adopted by many advocates of the postmodernist approach would have argued against many forms of more conventional empirical research as resting on outdated assumptions about the nature of the world and how it could be studied.

This stance meant that much of the writing on postmodernism was rather speculative and based on characterization of cultural and social changes (some of which was intensely thought-provoking) rather than detailed research into them. In my view this was not necessarily problematic provided that the theory was looked at in ways that recognized that such direct empirical research was not what it was seeking to achieve. However, it is possible to argue that the lack of detailed evidence for some of the key claims of the theory was problematic in the context of the generality of the claims made. Thus, if one of the important claims of the postmodern thesis was that new forms of culture were emerging that were often made up of fragments of old ones that were being brought together in ways that might have been seen as contradictory, and that such forms were associated with specific social groups, investigation of such an idea is on the face of it perfectly possible. There was an idea then that as part of cultural change the middle class was associated with the bringing together in often contradictory ways forms of culture that had previously been separated or associated with different groups. Most importantly, it was suggested that the boundaries between high and popular culture were being breached by the way in which sectors of the middle class were consuming both in ways that were new.

A significant paradox is that at the same time as this idea had gained some currency in some of the discussions around postmodernism, research was actually proceeding and being published that can be seen as examining some of these processes. This was the work that falls under the rubric of the omnivore thesis, which I introduced very briefly in an earlier chapter of this book. In my view this is therefore a significant intervention in the debate about cultural fragmentation in the broad sense and one of the reasons for my focus on it in this chapter stems from this view. However, there is another reason behind this analysis, as the idea and the research that has been carried out on it combine some of the key social and cultural processes that have been my focus in this book. Thus, as I will consider in this chapter the process of fragmentation and recombination of cultural forms that is involved in the omnivore thesis can be seen to involve processes of belonging, distinguishing and individualizing that have been key themes of my analysis. I will return to this theme during the course of my discussion in this chapter.

My analysis will proceed in the following way. First, I discuss in some detail the omnivore idea and the evidence for it. This will involve consideration of the context for the idea and the relationship between the idea of the omnivore and the univore that is an important part of the thesis. After characterizing the thesis I will consider initially the broader implications of the thesis in terms of what it means in terms of processes of social exclusion and distinction. This will lead me to discussion of the development of the omnivore thesis and how research that has been carried out to consider the thesis has led to revision of its claims. I will look at this through the following themes. First, there is the way that the thesis has been applied and investigated in societies other than the USA (where it originated). Second, I will consider how the thesis has been examined in a range of areas of cultural taste. Third, I will have more to say on the nature of the processes of distinction that are part of the omnivore thesis. Finally, I will consider the idea that the omnivore thesis can help to characterize forms of everyday talk about culture that intertwine processes of belonging, distinguishing and individualizing in important ways. I should say that for economy of exposition I adopt a similar approach in this chapter to that in other parts of the book. This means that I will often use a key study to exemplify an approach or important point rather than seeking to review all the studies that make the point. I have adopted this stance to make this discussion as 'punchy' as possible and to seek to illuminate as clearly as I can the key themes of my analysis.

The omnivore thesis: early statements and key themes

The omnivore thesis is a good example of an argument and investigation produced in the context of American sociology of culture, which has taken a fair while to be taken up seriously in the European study of culture. Moreover, the idea has primarily been researched within the context of the sociology of culture here and relatively little within cultural and media studies. As will be shown later, this has meant that some of the ways in which the concept has been investigated have taken particular directions. The reasons for this manner of take-up may have a number of causes, but some of the explanation may reside with the context in which the theory was developed as well as the methods used to investigate it.

The prime mover behind the idea, Richard Peterson, is well known as a researcher on the production of culture. Importantly, at the time that Peterson was developing his emphasis on the empirical investigation of the production of culture, a lot of culture and media studies was concerned with the analysis of texts in accord with a range of more general social and cultural theories. Moreover, what then developed was an analysis of the audience, rather than the production of cultural forms. It is only more recently that the swing of fashion has brought the production of culture more into focus. I suggest that this meant that the wider aspects of the omnivore thesis tended to be relatively neglected because of the relatively narrow interpretation of Peterson's work as concerned with the production of culture. In addition, Peterson's work on the production of culture does not start from Marxist principles and, given the influence of this perspective on some forms of media and cultural studies, this may have had some effect.

It is important to consider these points because as Peterson himself has argued, the omnivore thesis can be located within the overall framework of the production of culture thesis itself. Thus, in a co-authored and authoritative review of the production of culture thesis, Peterson and Anand (2004) argue that 'The production perspective was developed to better understand contexts in which cultural symbols are consciously created for sale, but it has been adapted to informal situations in which individuals and groups select among the symbolic products on offer and in the process create collective meanings and identities for themselves.' They term this the *auto-production of culture* (see also Peterson 2001) and argue that it counteracts the criticism of the production of culture perspective that it has neglected fan- and consumption-based studies of culture. This may not be as straightforward as they seem to suggest (see later). The production of culture perspective itself concentrates on six facets that condition the production of culture:

1   technology
2   law and regulation
3   industry structure
4   organization structure
5   occupational career
6   market.

For the purposes of this exposition it is not necessary to consider these processes further. In my view an excellent example of how this perspective can be applied fruitfully is found in Peterson's (1990a) classic article on the development of rock and roll.

Returning to the detail of the omnivore thesis, it is important that Peterson locates the initial findings in this respect in the context of a fairly simple distinction. He argues that much of the previous work on cultural taste had been concerned with the relationship between the elite and the mass in the context of mass society or mass culture theory. Thus, in the way in which he describes it the elite consumed or were characterized through the consumption of what has often been called high culture:

> [T]he hallmark of those at the top of the hierarchy according to the received elite-to-mass theory is patronizing the fine arts, displaying good manners, wearing the correct cut of clothes, using proper speech, maintaining membership in the better churches, philanthropic organizations and social clubs, and especially for the women of the class, cultivating all the attendant social graces. The term 'snob' applied to such people is of course pejorative.
>
> (Peterson 1992: 245)

In Peterson's view those in this position would resist low or popular cultural forms and practices. He argues that historically a number of different characterizations have been given of the culture of those at the 'lower' end of the social scale. Broadly, he suggests these fall into two main types: as restricted and tradition bound or as mass-like. Moreover, many theories have suggested that there has been some kind of move from a version of the former to the latter, as modes of massification of culture and society have occurred. Finally, there developed forms of culture between these extremes. These were often characterized as 'middlebrow'. A critical point is that these forms of culture were seen as separate. Thus in Peterson's argument those at the top 'will choose the fine arts and related leisure activities while shunning all others. Those near the middle will choose derivative works and activities, while those groups at the bottom will shun the fine arts and indiscriminately choose sensational and mass-oriented entertainments' (Peterson 1992: 246).

Peterson's work that argues against this 'received elite-to-mass theory' (1992: 246), had its origins in a rather different study that derived from the study of occupational groups and their cultures from within the production of culture approach described earlier. Despite this, in Peterson's view, the work that he carried out with Simkus (see Peterson and Simkus 1992) provided strong evidence that the received view was deficient. Based on 1982 data from the USA concerning the participation of adults in the arts, Peterson and Simkus defined 19 groups of occupations, ranging from higher cultural (including architects, lawyers, clergy and academics) to farm labourers. They then ranked these groups by the music that the members said that they liked best. The types of music were also ranked by occupational group. Basically they found that the highest occupational groups were far less exclusive in their tastes than the elite-to-mass theory would predict. While these groups had preferences for high culture forms of music, such as classical music, they also said that they liked country and western music, which in Peterson's view is 'the music with the lowest prestige of all' (1992: 248).

Moreover, the consideration of the occupational groups showed significant variation from what might have been expected, as some of the musical forms that should have been most popular with the lower groups turned out to be most liked by the higher groups:

> Indeed, the occupational groups at the top are much more likely to be high on liking these non-elite forms while the occupational groups at the bottom are likely to be low on the rate of liking them. Only one category of music, country and western, fits the predicted patterns, while three groups, mood music, big band and barber shop music, show just the opposite of the predicted ranking, and the other types of music show patterns that are quite mixed.
>
> (Peterson 1992: 249)

Peterson and Simkus were surprised at these results. They investigated further by exploring other 'non-elite leisure activities of the occupational groups' (Peterson 1992: 249). Again they found that the higher status groups had high levels of participation in what were defined as non-elite forms of activity. Thus, in their view the received elite-to-mass view did not capture the complexities of the situation that they were finding. They thought that the patterns of greater higher class participation in many of the activities considered could not be explained either by the fact that those at the top had more time (they did not as they worked longer hours) or by the fact that they were better off (as many of the activities were not dependent on significant investments of money). They do recognize that the data that they used for the study might not have captured some the cultural activities of the lower status groups – such as 'professional wrestling or betting on the numbers' (p. 252).

Peterson argues that these data provide evidence for two significant shifts that are occurring in cultural taste as related to occupational status groups. First, at the top, there is the move from the snob (the exclusive elitist) to the omnivore. Groups at the top liked what were considered to be 'low' forms of culture as well as the more elite forms. Further, and as will be seen later, this is an important point, 'status is gained by knowing about, and participating in (that is to say consuming) many if not all forms' (p. 252). Thus, knowing about a wide range of cultural forms actually is argued to enhance the position of the groups at the top end of the status hierarchy. In addition, groups at the top had sometimes communicated that they had found it difficult to choose one type of music that they liked best as they liked a range of music. Those at the top are moving from being elitist to be omnivores.

The second process concerns those at the lower end of the occupational spectrum. Peterson suggests that these groups cannot be seen as expressing a form of mass taste, as for example they do not spend more time watching television – the quintessential form of mass culture/taste. Indeed, Peterson, like other theorists before him, sees the term mass as a form of prejudice rather than an accurate description.[1] While the survey that they used could be used to characterize those at the lower end of the scale as culturally inactive, Peterson argues that the survey rather 'asked few questions about traditional working class leisure pursuits' (1992: 253), as has already been noted. Those at the bottom of the hierarchy were better able to choose their favourite type of music, which suggests that in Peterson's view they can be characterized as univore (thus neither mass-like nor omnivoric).

In conclusion to this summary argument, Peterson suggests that the patterning of taste, status and culture can be characterized in terms of two pyramids:

> In the first representing taste cultures there is at the top one elite taste constituting the cultural capital of the society and below it ever more numerous distinct taste cultures as one moves down the status pyramid. In the inverted pyramid representing concrete individuals and groups, there is at the top the omnivore who commands status by displaying any one of a range of tastes as the situation may require, and at the bottom is the univore who can display just one particular taste. This taste is nonetheless greatly valued by the univore because it is a way to assert an identity and to mark differences from other status groups at approximately the same level.
>
> (Peterson 1992: 254)

Peterson considers whether this omnivore/univore pattern is new or whether the received elite-to-mass view was wrong and had been based on inadequate research. His view is that the omnivore does actually represent the emergence of a new cultural pattern, but that there may always have been univores. The culture of lower end of society was misrepresented by studies in the past. He briefly introduces three explanations that might be offered for this new pattern. First, the idea of the superiority of high culture was affected by the 'realities of two World Wars' (p. 255). Second, that education has led to the decline of birth and cultural heritage as a basis for high status. Third, that social mobility entails that people continue to value their past culture. Peterson also argues that there are a number of processes in train that have made previously working-class forms of culture more 'respectable'. The processes that he identifies include, 'liberal education', the greater value placed on a range of cultural expressions, the way in which the media have exposed wider audiences to different forms of cultural expression and the commercial exploitation of a range of 'folk and ethnic-based' cultures. At this point in the development of the idea, Peterson could only speculate about the causes of the process and indeed more evidence was needed for the idea as a whole. This was recognized and more research called for.

As noted earlier, the original statement of the omnivore idea in 1992 was based on data gathered in 1982 and Peterson and Kern (1996) updated the discussion using data collected as part of a repeat of the same survey in 1992. To summarize, they found that in 1992 those at upper end of the social scale had become more omnivorous over the 10-year interval. Perhaps more importantly, however, the discussion took forward the consideration of the causes of these cultural changes. The discussion considers the impact of period effects (i.e. are people changing their tastes over time?) or cohort effects (i.e. are people with one set of tastes being displaced by younger members who have different tastes?). Peterson and Kern argue that both effects are present and that while there is some cohort replacement going on, in general 'high-brows of all ages are becoming more omnivorous' (p. 904). As the consideration of the findings had matured, it opened the way for more speculation on the causes of this 'empirical generalization' (Peterson and Kern 1996: 904).

One important overall point was made here, which was that the greater openness to a variety of cultural forms on the part of the omnivore did not mean that all cultural forms were appreciated equally. Thus, the patterns of cultural taste could still connect to forms of cultural and social distinction. It was simply that the cultural forms and perhaps the nature of these patterns had shifted over time. Furthermore, they make the point that it is not just what is consumed that matters in patterns of cultural taste, but *how* it is consumed. Thus, particular types of popular music may be consumed by omnivores in ways that were previously the case for 'classical' music as the relationships between genres and significant performers are analysed in ways that previously would have been thought inappropriate. Moreover, a literature has developed that facilitates such understanding and analysis (see Longhurst 2007).

Peterson and Kern (1996) suggest five factors that could explain the omnivore/univore shifts, which show important developments in thinking since the 1992 discussion. The five factors are: structural change, value change, art world change, generational politics and status group politics. Some of the processes considered under the heading of structural change encompass aspects considered earlier, such as educational shifts, but also introduced are social and geographical mobility, which could have mixed people who previously had separated tastes. Second, with respect to values there could be seen in general to be a greater overall tolerance and openness to the cultures and views of others. Thus, for example racist views and exclusions had in previous times been legitimated through science and had been widely accepted on this basis; however, such beliefs and the backing that they receive are now much less legitimate and cause far more controversy – 'It is now increasingly rare for persons in authority publicly to espouse theories of essential ethnic and racial group differences' (p. 905).

Third, the nature of culture or art worlds has changed. Thus as all forms of art become more commercialized, there arose a variety of cultural entrepreneurs who sought a variety of new modes of cultural and artistic expression. This has the effect of undermining the previous dominant value system that suggested that only one form of culture or art had artistic or moral credibility. This provides a new aesthetic sense of openness to different standards of what counts as good and these criteria shift over time. Fourth, there is generational politics. Peterson and Kern argue that prior to the development of rock and roll in the 1950s, young people were expected to move away for a taste for popular music as they grew up and matured. However, from the 1960s onwards the variety of music under the idea of rock became an 'alternative' form of culture rather than a stage to be moved through. This can be seen as of lasting importance, even if the precise nature of the music that falls under this heading has shifted over time.

Finally, there has been a shift in status group politics as popular culture has become more incorporated into dominant group culture. Thus, in the UK the Conservative Party leader, David Cameron, has been photographed wearing Converse trainers and Prime Minister Tony Blair proclaimed his rock and roll past. This leads Peterson and Kern (1996) to the general conclusion that: 'As highbrow snobbishness fits the needs of the earlier entrepreneurial upper-middle class, there also seems to be an elective affinity between today's new business-administrative class and omnivorousness' (p. 906).

In his earlier statements of the omnivore/univore thesis, Peterson tended to focus on the omnivore and the explanation for the trend towards the presence of omnivores in the dominant sections of society. This meant that there was relative neglect of the univores. This aspect of culture was addressed by Bryson (1997).

Bryson's consideration of univores is built on an earlier discussion where she examined taste through the important idea that as well as considering what forms people say that they *like*, attention should be paid to what they say that they dislike (Bryson 1996). This is important, as it potentially adds a finer grain to some of the discussions that focus on what people say they like. Thus in this study, Bryson shows that while there is an increased tolerance of the type that Peterson demonstrates through the omnivore thesis, there are limits as there are forms of culture that will not be tolerated. Thus, as she summarizes:

> I find that highly educated people in the United States are more music-ally tolerant, but not indiscriminately so. I provide evidence of class-based exclusion in that the genres most disliked by tolerant people are those most appreciated by people with the lowest levels of education.
>
> (Bryson 1996: 895)

Again this study was based on musical taste and the four most disliked genres were rap, heavy metal, country and gospel music. These were forms that are 'most strongly associated with low education' (p. 895). In continuity with this discussion, Bryson examined dislikes further. Her argument is that what she found confirms the idea of the univore initially discussed by Peterson. Thus she argues that:

> Lower status cultures are more likely than high status cultures to be defined around race, ethnicity, religious conservatism and geographic region. Musical dislikes are significantly more likely to be patterned around these identities at lower levels of education than they are other-wise.
>
> (Bryson 1997: 149)

While these findings are significant, Bryson argues that much more needed to be done to refine the understandings that had initially been theorized in the omnivore/univore thesis.

The omnivore thesis: wider applications and development of explanations

As Peterson and Anand (2004) show, the omnivore thesis has been subject to further investigation in a number of ways and in different countries. This has led to some refinement of the thesis as well as further examination of the causes of the social and cultural processes involved. In considering these developments, in accord with my approach in other parts of this book, I will focus on one significant representation that captures a number of aspects. Van Eijck (2000) offers an excellent example as he notes how 'Peterson's findings and interpretations regarding cultural patterns can be both affirmed and further specified if we compare them to other studies on the subject' (p. 208). Van Eijck recapitulates on some of the most important aspects of the omnivore thesis and argues that evidence for it can be found in newspaper and magazine reading in the Netherlands, where the number of people jointly reading newspapers at different levels such as 'quality' newspapers and 'gossip' magazines had increased. Thus, to transfer this finding to the British context it would be like more people reading *The Guardian* and *Hello!* While this finding is of significance as is the way that the thesis has been found to be transferable to other societies, I will focus on the further examinations for the development of omnivorous culture.

First, van Eijck examines the idea of social mobility, making sure that he separates diversity in individual taste from such diversity in a group. He rightly points out that these were not sufficiently distinguished in Peterson's formulations and that while they may often go together it is not necessarily the case. Thus, while the discussion of this in Peterson's argument tended to be at the individual level – socially mobile individuals retain an allegiance to forms of culture that they were brought up with – it might also be that the social composition of higher status groups has shifted due the overall trend to upward social mobility: 'Therefore, the diversity of tastes among the higher status groups may have come about as the sum of either omnivorous individual tastes, or from the diversity of tastes at the group level' (p. 212). Van Eijck suggests that both processes have occurred. Moreover, this process tends to accelerate.

The second important dimension that van Eijck explores is age. He argues that if the omnivore thesis is correct, then two main patterns should be found among the higher status groups: the traditional snobbish taste and the omnivore pattern. Given that the former is decreasing, it would be expected that the older people would exhibit the former and the younger ones the latter. Van Eijck explored this through a consideration of musical taste among Dutch people, using factor analysis. He found that while older generations were becoming more omnivorous, this was more likely to occur with younger people. Picking up on some other discussions of class he suggests that this is the culture of a new middle class.

This leads van Eijck to a significant consideration of the nature of the forms that are combined by the omnivores. Again it is important to point out that such patterns do not simply combine different types of culture randomly – that do not lack discrimination. This confirms the research undertaken by Bryson. The genre of world music is a good example of the type of combination that van Eijck, following Peterson (1990b) sees as a typical omnivore formations. This genre itself combines a diverse range of practitioners, so that 'it seems that the attraction lies in the musical experiment and the juxtaposition of diverse musical elements rather than in perfection within a well-defined genre' (p. 216). Van Eijck considers the different discourses that may be informing this pattern of taste and suggests that the omnivores are able to switch between different types of discourse. However, these processes also link very importantly to the types of distinction that I have considered in other parts of this book. Thus, van Eijck argues that world music, or the sorts of combination that maybe fall under this heading, might become 'the art music of the twenty-first century' (p. 219) and that appreciation of this type of music renders 'distinction because it is in accord with today's standard of what members of the upper-middle class are supposed to enjoy' (p. 219). Thus, the argument might be that omnivorousness is simply another mode of the pursuit of status on the part of relatively privileged groups. I will return to this point in more detail later, but it is important to point out that van Eijck argues that this may only be a part of the situation as not all cultural taste is to do with these processes. Thus as Mike Savage and I (Longhurst and Savage 1996) argued as well as seeking to impress others, cultural taste has as much to do with reassurance of the self – an argument picked up by van Eijck that I have further developed in this book. Moreover, Warde et al. (2000) argue that omnivorousness, if it is happening as a generalized process (and they suggest that there is mixed evidence for the UK) can be seen as much as reinforcing distinction as producing tolerance. In general, then, van Eijck shows that while Peterson's argument requires some degree of refinement, there are omnivorous processes happening in another society (in this case the Netherlands) and across other forms of culture (reading as well as music) and that the processes behind this can be further conceptualized.

Other studies have continued to explore the omnivore idea. Thus, for example, work on Spain (e.g. Sintas and Álvarez 2002) has found that omnivores are present, but does not necessarily show that the patterns of omnivoric culture are replacing the highbrow form. Like other studies, the omnivore type culture is related to increased levels of education and (younger) age. In the UK, Warde et al. (1999) have considered the thesis with respect to eating out. There is now a developing pattern of research that is exploring the pertinence of the omnivore thesis. While this has led to refinement of the idea, the basic parameters have been found in a number of different societies. It is important to note that these studies have nearly always worked with quantitative data and are using quantitative data analysis techniques of increasing sophistication in examining the patterns of cultural taste and distinction. On a number of levels this is to be welcomed as it provides important ways of carrying out cross-national studies and has led to revision and increased sophistication in the omnivore idea. However, there is a danger that precisely this sophistication and indeed the ways in which the quantitative papers that discuss the omnivore idea are written will lead to lack of attention outside a fairly specialized group. The implications of this danger are that some of the insights are neglected by those working in different research traditions (such as cultural and media studies) and with different modes of analysis that are based on more qualitative analysis and modes of critical speculation. As I have argued, and it is one of the basic themes behind this book, such gulfs are to be avoided. To examine this point, I now turn to other ways of thinking the omnivore/univore idea that show how such connections can be made.

Cultural taste: qualitative consideration and modes of speech

In a number of papers Holt (e.g. 1995, 1997a, 1997b, 1998) argued in ways that can be seen as making a number of interconnected points. Thus his work shows that it is important not just to consider what people say they do (often in response to relatively crude questions about taste in surveys), but the practices that they engage in. Thus, what people mean by saying that they like one form of music rather than another may vary considerably. For example, liking something may mean listening to it when it comes on the radio or buying every album (and bootlegs) by an artist and reading every book and article written about them. There is a danger that these sorts of difference are collapsed under headings of likes and dislikes. In these senses, as Holt (1997b) explores, practices as well as objects require exploration. Moreover the combinations of what people say that they like are significant. Thus, while as considered earlier, it appears that forms of music that are brought together under the heading of a genre of 'world' are actually very different (and indeed on a number of levels they are), there is a pattern here and the forms are considered in similar sorts of ways. Thus they are seen often as some kind of authentic modes of expression of a 'traditional' culture that fits in well with ideas of authenticity that have been pervasive in modes of distinction in rock music in the western world.

On the basis of such points, Holt argues ultimately for an agenda of consideration of cultural taste and distinction that recognizes four themes:

1   Consider culture in ways that recognizes specificities. Thus, for example asking people what genres of music they like (or dislike) may completely miss the variation in a genre. Thus most musical genres are rather wide (and, indeed, vary over time at least partly in response to commercial decisions) and it is perfectly possible to like one form of country music and dislike another. Furthermore, these tastes are likely to be patterned as the omnivore likes some country artists but not others and the univore likewise.

2   In a related fashion, the meanings of a cultural object and practice require consideration in context. In a memorable comment, Holt (1997a) captures this point when he argues that: 'The social classificatory consequences of a 55-year-old Anglo-Saxon woman declaring her appreciation for rap and rattling off several favourite artists has entirely different semiotic value from Mexican- or African-American youth doing the same' (p. 118).

3   It is important that discussions look across a range of what Holt terms 'consumption fields' looking at practices, but also reading, listening to music, watching films and TV, and so on.

4   He argues that ethnographic consideration is of importance, to get behind some of the relative bluntness of survey instruments.

These sorts of point can be considered further.

When more qualitative data on cultural taste is considered through the lens of the omnivore/univore thesis some significant points arise. Thus, in such work with Eamonn Carrabine (Carrabine and Longhurst 1999) and Mike Savage and Gaynor Bagnall (Savage et al. 2005), I found that with respect to music, middle-class youth and adults expressed what can be termed an 'omnivorous refrain' with respect to initial discussions of taste. Thus, in a focus group and interviews with respect to the former and interviews with the latter, people tended to answer a general question about what music they liked by stressing that they appreciate a wide variety of different forms. However, as discussion proceeded, this position was often qualified in ways that showed that actually their taste was not as wide as they had initially expressed or that they had a pretty clear pattern of likes and dislikes. This suggests that with respect to music, this kind of omnivoric refrain has become a dominant pattern of speech – in some sense, what these sorts of people are expected to say – and indeed a legitimate form of expression. However, the situation with respect to other forms of culture varied. It is especially pertinent to consider the case of television. Here the initial response was very different. People certainly did not in general say that they liked all television or even that they had wide taste; rather, the opposite was the case. They sought to narrow what they said they liked through emphasizing, first, that they did not watch much television and, second, that when they did it was focused on news and documentary programmes. Thus, with respect to television people clearly sought to distance themselves from a mass medium that is still talked about in terms that stress its 'addictive' qualities and that still tends to be devalued culturally. It is something to be as spoken about as to be resisted.

The group that we found that differed most from these patterns was a section of the middle class that resided in the 'trendy' suburb of Chorlton in Manchester (Savage et al. 2005). These people expressed their 'imagined cosmopolitanism' in modes of elective belonging (see Chapter 5) that emphasized cultural pluralism and the ability to enjoy 'high' and 'popular' culture. In many ways they were classic omnivores and were relaxed about expressing this with respect to music and television (as well as other forms of culture). Again, how 'deep' this omnivorousness goes is debatable and our argument was that actually this group was less cosmopolitan than their self-perception might suggest. In a number of respects, this reinforces the points made earlier about the need to look at taste in specific context and to recognize that patterns of taste will differ with respect to different forms of culture, even if for certain people they come together. Moreover, these patterns can be clearly related to patterns of distinction.

Skeggs (2004: 144) argues very clearly that in many ways, if omnivoric culture exists (and there are empirical qualifications and refinements to be made) then it can be seen as a strategy on the part of sections of the middle class to reinforce their already powerful position. As she states:

> So time, knowledge, information, bodily investment, mobility across cultural boundaries and social networking all constitute resources for the formation of the new middle-class omnivorous self. The cultural omnivore, therefore, enables the middle-classes to re-fashion and re-tool themselves.

(Skeggs 2004: 144)

Thus, in this view as a group and as individuals the middle class continues to accumulate capital. For Skeggs, then the middle-class omnivore involves an individual who is accumulative. He or she adds patterns of culture to their identity, even if they do not necessarily go into these in depth (see, for example, Erickson 1996). This view that omnivorousness is a strategy to reinforce class distinction and differential class power is also advanced by Sayer (2005). Drawing on the work of Skeggs and Warde et al., he argues that:

> Attempts at mixing downwards seem to imply a refusal of advantage and symbolic violence, raising the obvious question: 'What's in it for them?' The outsider may merely want to pass as having a different class position from her own out of self-interest, to gain access to the internal goods of other social classes, to be a social chameleon in order to get the best of all social worlds.

(Sayer 2005: 173)

However, while concurring with what can therefore be seen as the downside of omnivorousness, in accord with his other arguments (see Chapter 6), Sayer also suggests that there may be other more positive aspects of this process. Thus while these shifts in culture and taste cannot simply be seen as promoting greater tolerance and openness and indeed there is a significant aspect of promotion of new forms of distinction, the idea of crossing class boundaries should not be seen in simple negative terms.

Conclusion

While, in many respects, the picture is more mixed than Peterson's initial arguments would suggest, in that both the extent of omnivorousness and the nature of the shift in power and status that it represents have been debated, it is clear that there is a pattern of social and cultural change here that is significant. In terms of the context in which I set this discussion at the beginning of the chapter, the analysis of the omnivore idea suggests that the modes of cultural fragmentation (and reconstitution) involve processes of change that can be theorized in terms of shifts in the nature of modernity. Indeed, during the course of the height of the debate about postmodernity, there were arguments that new forms of postmodern culture were associated with the new middle class and this became a sub-theme in the debate (see, for example, Pfeil 1990). A key point then is that modes of social change represented in that debate have clear significance, even if the attempt to unify them under the banner of 'postmodernism' was ultimately too crude. It is important, I suggest, to pay attention to precisely these shifts. An important point about the omnivore thesis in this context is that it rests on some detailed evidence about cultural change. In this sense it has been a real stimulus to attention to cultural patterns that do not simply rest on speculation. This is of major importance, as we now have a significant level of evidence about cultural patterns that would not have existed otherwise. More of this work, which also recognizes the importance of qualitative work and context, can only be of benefit.

It is also important to recognize that the media drenching of ordinary life that is a core theme of this book is an important driver and resource for the spread of more omnivorous forms of culture. Thus, it is now possible to have access to a greater range of cultural products in a reasonably straightforward way than ever before. These may be, for example, films made by European art house cinema directors or past series of popular TV shows, as well as 24-hour TV. This is important, as these resources mean that there is much more available to provide the bases for audience and performance activity in ordinary life.

Note

1 The most significant was Raymond Williams who argued that 'There are in fact no masses; there are only ways of seeing people as masses' (Williams 1963: 289).

9 Enthusing

In Chapter 4, I outlined the spectacle/performance paradigm and in the rest of this book so far, I have sought to show the general relevance of the spectacle/performance paradigm for the analysis of ordinary life in advanced capitalist societies. In a number of ways this book seeks to advance the agenda of two earlier ones (Abercrombie and Longhurst 1998; Savage et al. 2005) and I would argue that it has done this, but some of the particulars of the arguments require some further development. There are two broad reasons for this. First, it is important to return to some of the specific arguments about audience processes that led to the more general conclusions of this book as they offer concrete evidence about social and cultural change. Second, since the original formulation of the spectacle/performance paradigm much new work on fans and audiences has been produced. Some of this has been integrated into the discussion in Chapter 4, however, in this chapter I take this discussion forward on a number of fronts. This discussion will intertwine evidence that has been produced from empirical studies of audience processes and fan activity, as well as drawing on the theoretical innovation that has taken place on the basis of that substantial research.

Much current research has considered fandom in a range of ways. As *Audiences* argued (Abercrombie and Longhurst 1998), there is still some confusion over different definitions of fandom and we proposed a typology to overcome this. While some authors have used the typology and some have criticized it, I still maintain its core utility (see Chapter 4). While we used the idea of 'enthusiasm' to examine a particular point on the audience continuum, I will, in much of this chapter, use the idea of enthusing to capture the idea of some degree of investment in forms of culture be they directly media related or not. This will enable me to compare evidence on similar processes across a range of practices.

Another key aim of this chapter is to examine the place of what might be called excessive or better *extraordinary* aspects of ordinary life. I do not want to draw a hard line between ordinary and extraordinary forms of life and culture. Rather, I argue that what might be thought to be extraordinary attachments and forms of activity are part of ordinary life. This means that there is a fluidity to the way in which we move from one form of attachment to another.

This may happen very quickly and be marked by very little change or it may involve a significant journey and the marking of an event as extra special. Moreover, the increased power and salience of the extraordinary in a number of ways are one of the key ways in which ordinary life is itself changing, as the general processes that I have described facilitate a more spectacular and performative society. It is important to recognize that this does not mean that some of the typically thought of forms and aspects of fandom are necessarily becoming more salient. Thus, I would want to argue that approaches to celebrity (e.g. Rojek 2001), while they have much to offer in characterizing fame and stardom and their roles in advanced capitalist societies tend still to pathologize fandom, because of where they start (i.e. with the celebrity). Moreover, studies of fans by their very focus have a tendency to separate fans from the activities of others. By their research, attention to excess and, for example, 'cult media' there is a danger than fandom becomes in one sense theorized as part of ordinary life but in other ways bracketed from it. Thus, I seek to mobilize neither celebrity studies nor fandom research in these ways. However, I will seek to use relevant empirical and theoretical studies to develop the characterization of enthusing in ordinary life.

In accord with some of the overall arguments of this book, I locate this discussion within the points that I have already made concerning the overall significance of performing and audiencing in ordinary life and how the interrelation of belonging, distinguishing and individualizing processes run through those of enthusing. Moreover, through this route, I seek to explore three key aspects of the literature on audience and fan processes: the social, the psychological and the spatial. I have already considered the interconnection of these processes via concepts such as 'elective belonging' and scene, which have the potential to bring these aspects together. This chapter takes that integrating discussion forward. Specifically, I begin the discussion by offering an overview of what is at stake in this discussion, drawing on two rather different sources, one an overview of 'reception studies' (Staiger 2005) and the other a study of contemporary football (Sandvoss 2003). This will be followed by an examination of two of the most significant attempts to develop an overall theory of fandom that have been produced to date (Hills 2002; Sandvoss 2005). This leads to discussions of media and society that have sought to theorize ritual and space in new ways to show the particular powers of the media. In this section, I consider the work of Couldry (2000b, 2003) in particular, having drawn on some of his other work (Couldry 2000a) in my consideration of the idea of the ordinary. This will lead in the final part of the chapter to some consideration of the nature of reality TV, especially in connection to Couldry's (2005) idea of the extended audience, which is an argument that considers further the concept of the diffused audience. Through this process, I seek to further the analysis of ideas of audiencing, spectacle and the dynamic between the ordinary and the extraordinary.

Processes of reception and sport

In her comprehensive overview of reception studies, Staiger (2005) clearly shows that the field deploys psychological and sociological theories (which have been drawn on in the spectacle/performance paradigm). Defining her topic in a broad way, Staiger uses the terms 'spectator, reader, viewer and audience interchangeably' (p. 3). While there are a number of specific theories that 'reception' research draws on, Staiger identifies three broad lines of psychological work: behaviourism, psychoanalysis and cognitive psychology (pp. 4–6). Behaviourism has been influential on the earlier days of audience research (see the discussion in *Audiences*), but its models of direct media effects on individuals are now little discussed in academic research. Psychoanalytical forms of research have been of particular influence in the study of film and cinema, where discussions of the construction or interpellation of the spectator by filmic texts have been much explored. Cognitive and more social forms of psychology have been of influence on more contemporary audience research, for example, on work on British continuous serials (Livingstone 1990). An emphasis in this kind of work is on how 'individuals develop schemata (mental scripts, frameworks, prototypes, templates) from social experience' (p. 6). Staiger identifies two broad types of social theory: functionalism and conflict theory. The differences between these social theories are well known. The former concentrates on issues of integration and the function of particular phenomena in contributing to forms of consensus; the latter on conflict and dispute. Somewhat paradoxically, both can end up with a focus on how the media influence audiences towards a form of consensus, either 'real' or 'imposed' in some sense.

Staiger's account of fandom draws heavily on Henry Jenkins (1992). Jenkins identified five processes of fan activity (see Abercrombie and Longhurst 1998: 126), which can be summarized in the ideas that fans are 'skilled or competent in different mode of production and consumption; active in their interaction with texts and in their production of new texts; and communal in that they construct different communities based on their links to the programmes they like' (Abercrombie and Longhurst 1998: 127). To this approach, Staiger adds a point that is of significance for the argument of this book. This is that fans' 'partialities' are extended into 'everyday living'. These might involve collecting, naming children after favourite characters, visiting spaces and places associated with the object of fan investment, and so on.

The sorts of theory that are identified by Staiger as of general importance to audiences are applicable to fans. However, as she argues, explanations often draw on several different streams of explanation. This is important as:

> The variety of explanations for fan behavior is exciting, for the variety of behaviors is also wide. Fans display interpretations and effects (activities) in their most observable form. While the phenomenon of fandom exceeds the typical, likely it points toward the more silent spectator – although probably almost everyone has been a fan in some way.
>
> (Staiger 2005: 114)

These ideas can be further explored through a concrete example. At the end of *Audiences* (Abercrombie and Longhurst 1998), we conducted a brief examination of how contemporary football could be explored in the context of the idea of the diffused audience and the SPP. Aspects of this analysis have impacted on subsequent and far more detailed and sophisticated analyses of sport, such as the work of Crawford (2004) discussed in Chapters 3 and 4, who argues that:

> The proliferation of mass media resources, consumer goods and the increase in social performativity, have extended an individual's ability to form links with multiple fluid communities in their everyday lives. In particular, due to the decline of many 'traditional' communities, such as those based upon locality and extended family networks, other sources of community, such as sport fan culture, offer individuals the opportunity to 'buy into' a sense of community and 'play out' their roles as active participants within these.
>
> (Crawford 2004: 159)

It is in this light that the work of Sandvoss (2003) can be considered. This is a book that offers a range of insights into the contemporary football experience in a number of ways. I shall focus at this point on two main strands in Sandvoss' argument. These concern the nature of identity and place and space in the context of globalization.

Sandvoss (2003: 27) introduces a thesis of significant importance when he argues that:

> My hypothesis is the following. Football fans – through consumption in a supermediated world – communicate a projection of themselves. The main object of consumption in football fandom and hence the crucial, if not exclusive, vehicle for this act of articulation (and projection) is the football club, as fans as consumers of performances constitute an audience engaged with a text.

The identification with a club becomes a significant part of the fan's personality. It is important (as with Crawford's earlier argument) that this identification does not depend on locality: 'Fans who started following a team for the colour of their shirts were as likely to be committed followers of a team as those born in the vicinity of the same club. To all these fans, regardless of the origins of their fandom, clubs serve as spaces of self-projection' (p. 35).

These processes are exemplified by the way in which fans use 'we' in relationship to the club. For Sandvoss, therefore, these forms of fandom are 'an extension of the self' (p. 38). He develops this idea of the extended self of fandom via the work of McLuhan, but offers the idea that these forms of fandom are both projections of the self and reflections: 'The object of fandom is therefore a reflection of the fan. What fans are fascinated by is their own image, an extension of themselves' (p. 39). Fans' bond is based on an extension of who they are. The club is a reflection, but Sandvoss argues that they do not recognize it. As clubs change, argues Sandvoss, these changes are incorporated back into the self. So as changes affect the club or are driven by the club, so the fans are able to bring these changes into their own personality and their everyday lives. However, this is not necessarily a straightforward process as the club and the world may be changing in ways that are not welcomed by the fan. This causes tension that the fan may seek to reconcile. Moreover, Sandvoss develops this argument in the context of our previous arguments about performance, audience and spectacle. Fans seek an audience for these performances of the extended self (Sandvoss 2003: 42–3):

> In the following extract, two fans discuss the degree to which they themselves succeed in becoming performers on a mass mediated stage:
>
> *Harald*: All right, I like to watch all the surroundings [on television].
>
> *Thomas*: I watched the game on DSF yesterday again and what do they show? Two brain-dead people standing around somewhere, who applaud. But they didn't show our choreography.
>
> *Harald*: Against Monaco you could see the choreography, but that was coincidence.
>
> (Harald and Thomas, Bayer Leverkusen fans)

Thus, in seeking an audience, they have become performers. In addition, Sandvoss argues that the audience of this performance itself decays as with Echo in the Narcissus myth. In these ways fandom as attachment involves processes of extension and reflection that make audiences performers and which have major implications for the self. I take up these arguments further later. The second key aspect of Sandvoss' argument concerns diffusion, globalization and place.

Sandvoss explores the nature of communities as they are formed around football. As I have discussed earlier, there is often an assumption in more simple forms of the globalization thesis that community would be obliterated by globalizing processes. However, as I have considered, what is actually happening is that the nature of community is changing. With particular attention to place, I have theorized this via concepts of elective belonging and scene so far. Sandvoss' consideration of the specific form of culture reinforces this emphasis. His emphasis is on the 'voluntary' nature of contemporary community: 'Fandom, as I have argued, can now be forged by drawing on an endless variety of texts originating in modern mass media and first of all television. This is not to argue that identification with local clubs has ceased, but that it has become *optional*' (p. 91, my emphasis). Sandvoss uses the idea of imagined community to theorize the way that fans think about their connections to other fans of the same club. For Sandvoss, considered through the example of football, and using Tomlinson (1999), locales are 'complex cultural spaces' (p. 92). As the fan base for the larger clubs widens globally so such clubs have 'local' and 'global' fans. This then involves a reconstruction of what it means to have local rivalries. Sandvoss discusses the example of Chelsea fans living in Norway who see 'Manchester United, Liverpool or other London clubs as their local rivals' (p. 100). These are not necessarily the traditional rivals for Chelsea, as: 'The symbolic space of shared competition emerges as more important in the construction of self-identity and group membership than the actual geographical place inhabited by fans' (p. 100). It should be recognized that such forms of fandom are no less 'authentic' than those associated with 'traditional' patterns of residence. Similar points with respect to other sports are made by Crawford (2004).

Another important part of Sandvoss' argument concerns the nature of football stadia as providing spaces for identity, community and identification. In the context of theories of postmodernity and standardization of consumer activity, Sandvoss considers the changing nature of football stadia, which now 'offer a theme-parkesque range of services' (p. 122). There has been a tendency in much of the literature that because of their similarities and blandness, people do not form attachments to such places. However, Sandvoss shows that this is actually not the case. Football fans felt forms of belonging for these places (p. 133). However, television is also important in offering the opportunity for the reconstitution of such relationships. There has been a tendency to suggest that television affects community and identity negatively, but Sandvoss' broad point (and it is a key point of other fan studies as well) is that it actually reconstitutes such relationships. Of course, this may have negative aspects, but then so did 'traditional' identifications and communities. Furthermore, because so much football is now consumed via television, this offers further opportunities for fans to project their identities into different places and spaces.

There are in Sandvoss' argument some clear downsides to these developments and as football becomes more standardized and postmodern (or, better, hypermodern), 'a growing number of fans find it difficult to maintain the common ground of self-reflection and identification with their object of fandom. As football embodies and expresses tendencies of rationalized and hyperreal production, fans opposing such changes are confronted with landscapes they cannot integrate into their construction of fandom' (p. 162). However, while this may be true for some fans, it is not necessarily the most common experience.

Fundamentally then Sandvoss explores a dynamic between the way that changes in culture, in this case football as it becomes a transformed mediatized and consumerist form opens the way for new projections and projects of identity, but also how football as a representation becomes freer of the original live event:

> The televisual representation of football thus threatens to transform into its own simulacrum: a copy, endlessly duplicated, to which there is no original. In this sense, football has entered a postmodern stage. Television has set the pace for the transformation of stadia into placeless environments which seek to emulate the televisual representation of football, not shape it. Consequently, to many fans football on television has replaced the actual game as the point of reference.
>
> (Sandvoss 2003: 173)

The extension that Sandvoss speaks of thus double-edged in his view and the increased narcissism of consumption can cause identity problems. He therefore does not celebrate this situation.

In this section, I have sought to consider, in the context of audience studies and a specific consideration of fandom, what can be seen in broad terms as psychological and sociological processes and to pull out some of the ways in which such themes have been explored in some path-breaking work on sport. In the next section, I seek to draw out some further general lessons from this sort of approach.

Theories of fandom

Drawing on the discussion so far, in this section I consider two of the most important syntheses and overall theories of fan studies that have been produced so far. The work of Hills (2002) and Sandvoss (2005) will be discussed through the following themes: capitals and distinction; place and space; psychology, psychoanalysis and the theory of the self; texts and their limits. I begin with a short comment on terminology.

While, as stated earlier, I use the term enthusing to head this chapter, I still beneath this remain committed to the distinction between fan, cultist and enthusiast theorized in *Audiences* (Abercrombie and Longhurst 1998). This terminology was criticized by Hills (2002), who says that: 'It seems faintly unhelpful to produce a taxonomy in which the definition of "fan" is at odds with the use of the term in almost all other literature in the field' (p. ix). One answer to this is to point to the potential problems of using the 'the term "cult fan" interchangeably with "fan" ' (p. x), as this seems to limit and reduce analysis. Another answer is to suggest that it may indeed be helpful to use a new terminology if the retheorization captures something that previous accounts have tended to obscure through their own terminological uses and the effects that this has. A version and development of this point are more fully argued by Sandvoss (2005).

After noting that on the surface there are indeed some issues with this 'taxonomy', as for example few football fans would describe themselves as 'cultists', using the term fan instead, however, for Sandvoss this is a 'problem of terminology, not substance' (p. 31). Thus again with respect to football and music fans, Sandvoss argues that:

> In quantitative terms, it is important to note that the continuum between fans, cultists and enthusiasts is a pyramid instead of a linear continuum. Box office takings, audience ratings and market research on music or football fandom all illustrate that fans that regularly follow the fan text in its mass-mediated form outnumber those attending live events or conventions, or even become producers in their own right. 'Fans' thus account for by far the largest segment of the fan continuum, with a substantially smaller number of cultists and even fewer enthusiasts.
>
> (Sandvoss 2003: 32)

Sandvoss points out that the distinctions also capture important differences of focus between groupings, as well as allowing consideration of the similarities between them. Importantly, he suggests that this then relates to the 'potential for empowerment and emancipation in fandom' (p. 32). Moreover, for Sandvoss this relates to identity and social processes:

> In other words, fandom and the power relations within fandom are based upon the capacity of popular texts, whether produced by the media industry or fans, to carry meaning that articulates fans' identity and their objective and subjective position within society.
>
> (Sandvoss 2003: 32)

An important way in which fan studies have sought to consider the social is via the work on Bourdieu.

Bourdieu and fandom

As Hills and Sandvoss show, Bourdieu's work on distinction and capitals has been influential on studies of fandom and in aspects of contemporary work on youth subcultures. However, Hills argues in suggestive ways that this work has been limited in at least two ways. First, Bourdieu has a particular understanding of cultural capital, as legitimate education and knowledge of fine art and so on that has to be expanded and rethought in the context of the modes of cultural capital that are significant for fans. While the literature on fandom has done this, it still shows the effects of this sort of Bourdieu emphasis. In particular, and in a second related fashion, this literature has tended relatively to neglect social capital, as Bourdieu tends also to do. He also argues that the 'calculative' model proposed by Bourdieu has difficulty in explaining why people become involved in fandom at all.

This line of argument has much in common with that used by Devine (2004) in the work on education discussed in Chapter 7 and more general critique by Sayer (2005) considered in Chapter 6. Thus, Devine also rejects instrumentalist accounts to show how it is the interaction of capitals (and the fact that this does not guarantee successful outcomes) that are important. Hills, therefore, can be read as offering an argument that shows that the interaction between capitals is pertinent and that this discussion has also to be linked to wider considerations of motivations and identity. This therefore requires sociological and psychological (or psychoanalytical) dimensions as I have argued throughout this chapter so far.

An important part of Bourdieu's work that has also been taken into fan studies is the idea of distinction. On one level, fan activities can be interpreted as involving distinction in a fairly orthodox sense, thus using the work of Thomas (2002) on *Inspector Morse* and *The Archers* as one example, Sandvoss is able to argue that: 'There is substantial evidence in support of an understanding of fan tastes as yet another segment of the process of distinction through consumption, in line with an orthodox reading of Bourdieu's analysis in studies which have correlated the choice of the object of fandom to fans' class position' (2005: 35). However, in addition to such class differences other lines of cleavage appear in fandom that mean that Bourdieu's account requires refinement. This has involved continuing and renewed attention to distinction and hierarchies within fandom and a number of studies have now deployed such an approach, which reinforces the need to consider the interconnections between different forms of capital. It also shows how these debates require connection to issues of identity.

Space, place and fandom

I will explore this issue in further detail in the next section of this chapter via some important work by Couldry; however, Sandvoss (2005) clearly illustrates the way in which space and place interact in fan processes. Thus, in one respect, as with other considerations of the mass media in this book, the texts and processes of fandom are placeless. The same episode of a TV series can be watched in very different spaces and places around the world. Likewise, they are also in many respects relatively timeless. By recording episodes or purchasing/hiring a boxed set, TV can be viewed at different times. These points are well worn. However, what is perhaps increasingly significant is how these practices are placed. As Sandvoss says:

> Places of fandom thus take on a dual meaning. On the one hand, they incorporate tendencies to placelessness for their other-directedness with respect to the fan text; on the other, they are transformed into the territorial focus of the individual and group identities.
>
> (Sandvoss 2005: 66)

Sandvoss argues that physical spaces become important for fans, in that as the literature shows fans want to visit the places where series are made (or shot on location) or the places that are of particular significance with respect to the star. However, it is important to note that these practices can be differentiated with respect to the distinction between fan, cultist and enthusiast and the importance of the place to the object of attention. Thus, someone might be fanlike with respect to *The X-Files* in that they have watched every episode, but have no desire to visit Vancouver, where much of the show was filmed. Likewise, there may be little spatial referent that makes sense in relation to a particular star. Thus, for example, Rodman (1996) shows very well that Graceland as a particular site for Elvis cultists/enthusiasts to visit is dependent on the fact that Elvis chose to live in this one place for the best part of 20 years of his life; that it is accessible and a visible (rather than hidden) place; and that a tourist industry has developed around it. In this sense, placeness is reinforced rather than played down. Other stars, as Rodman argues are much less connected with specific places. They may be associated with a city, if they are pop stars, but may be reclusive if they are Hollywood actors and so on.

Sandvoss argues that this sort of placing of fandom (or what I call in broad terms, enthusing) contributes to the production of a sense of home. This sort of argument, which elaborates in some respects on those mounted by Silverstone (1994) and Morley (2000), is very suggestive. However, in my view it can be best theorized through the idea of scenic elective belonging that I have deployed in other parts of this book. There are several reasons for this. First, these ideas retain a focus on place, but allow the introduction and consideration of a number of social and cultural processes that produce the effect of belonging. Second, it emphasizes the action of people in producing the sense of belonging. The danger with some versions of home, in my view, is that they retain aspects of a simple version of belonging as dependent solely on period of residence. Third, the idea of scene, as has been argued earlier, facilitates consideration of the way that media enter into processes of performing and audiencing. These ideas, again as has been suggested at many points in my analysis so far, also facilitate considerations of the processes of identity constitution and reconstitution. The literature on fandom, as I have already introduced in this chapter, also has important things to say on this topic.

Identity and subjectivity

Hills (2002) has argued that fan studies need to include significant attention to what he terms the 'affective play' of fandom. He emphasizes the creativity and emotional import of fandom to those who are engaged in the variety of fan activities. While both of these aspects have been addressed in earlier work on fans, especially by Grossberg (1992) in his account of affect, Hills argues that Grossberg's account is limited by its inattention to the playful aspects of fandom and the fluidity of the boundaries of the self and society. Grossberg's account does not make fan activity sound like it is much fun. Hills argues that the theory of affective play is transgressive in a number of ways, as it transgresses boundaries between different disciplines, that between emotion and affect, and that between affect and cognition (p. 93). Hills argues that a more 'subjective' cultural studies is required.

The way in which Hills approaches this is to develop the work of Winnicott (see also Silverstone 1994 and Harrington and Bielby 1995), while, however, drawing much from these previous deployments of Winnicott. The basic idea is that TV acts as a transitional object and that attachments are formed through this process. However, Hills argues that:

> A distinction needs to be made between the transitional object-proper (an actual physical object which the child both finds and creates, originally through fantasies of destruction) and the cultural field which is said to displace the transitional object through the natural decathexis of the object-proper. But in neither account is such a distinction drawn.
>
> (Hills 2002: 106)

For Hills, then, a key issue is how the process of connection to a transitional object as a 'private' act in childhood is translated into cultural and social aspects of later life. His example of this helps: 'Or one might add, from the private experience of playing with a *Star Wars* toy figure to a communal pleasure in attending *Star Wars* conventions' (p. 108). He thus deploys the idea of the secondary transitional object to account for this process. The secondary transitional object 'has not altogether surrendered its affective charge and private significance for the subject, despite having been recontextualised as an intersubjective cultural experience' (p. 109). In addition, 'the secondary transitional object enters a cultural repertoire which "holds" the interest of the fan and constitutes the subject's symbolic project of self' (p. 109). Thus, objects of attention and significance may or may not be retained depending on condition and context, but also in Hills' argument because of the nature of the text itself. Thus those that appeal to different age groups from the beginning are more likely to be retained, such as *Doctor Who*. These texts also have a degree of openness that allows them to do different things for a person at different points of the life course depending on their shifting and developing interests. Thus, I watched *Doctor Who* differently in the early 1960s, as a sometimes frightened child, from how I watched as a teenager in the 1970s with friends, to how it engages me now with my own sons and partner as someone with knowledge of fan, audience, social and cultural theory (and the text has changed markedly over that time as well). It still remains of some, albeit differential, importance.

Hills also draws attention to these processes of life shifts in significance of fan objects with his idea of autoethnography. While there is a danger of collapsing into complete solipsism in using one's own attachments to consider fan biography, in my view there is value in such processes especially when viewed in the light of the more social/cultural tracing of life shifts in the work of Gauntlett and Hill (1999) as discussed in Chapter 7. Thus, while Hills usefully applies these ideas to his own biography and shifting attachments to media, this could also be done to some depth through the analysis of media-centred life narrative accounts. This is an area that remains relatively unexplored. Hills offers important ideas concerning the development of the self and how investments can playfully shift over time. Ideas concerning identity are also further considered by Sandvoss.

Key aspects of the general approach proposed by Sandvoss have already been introduced via the discussion of the example of football. Thus, he argues that media operate as an extension of the self. Fandom and audience processes are therefore fundamentally narcissistic. Sandvoss arrives at this position through the critique of other psychological and psychoanalytical approaches. He suggests that three forms have been influential: Freudian, Kleinian and those derived (as in Silverstone and Hills) from the work of Winnicott. For Sandvoss, in broad terms all these approaches run into the problem of the social dimensions of fandom and play. However, Freudian theories 'nevertheless provide a useful starting point to explore fan fantasies constituted in the field of tension between id and superego' (2005: 94). While Klein's work facilitates consideration of 'processes of projection and introjection, whereby the object of fandom becomes an extension of aspects of the fan's self, as well as vice versa' (p. 94). The problem is that it can lead to a 'pathologization of fans' (p. 94). The Winnicott-influenced work is important as it 'underlines the important function of fandom as a realm of negotiation between inner and external realities, and thus as a source of both pleasure and security', however, it 'needs to be counterbalanced by an analysis of the content and framing of such play' (p. 94). Thus, in many respects Sandvoss is building on the approach represented by Hills.

In arguing for the way in which the self is narcissistically extended via connections to the media, it is important to recognize that Sandvoss is not simply asserting that the audience and the fans are self-centred in a narrow way. As he suggests, the issues that this raises in the way in which this relationship between self and other works can form the basis for action, critique and change. Thus, deriving his discussion from the work of Marcuse, he argues that this process can 'bear on the potential to challenge forms of existing social organization' (p. 122). However, the extent to which this is the case depends in his argument on the nature of texts.

Texts

It has long been a truism of studies of fandom that the texts are relatively open, in the sense that texts are polysemic. They are open to a variety of interpretations and can be reworked to form new texts and practices. The nature of these texts and practices is one of the key surprises that affect outsiders to fandom when first confronted with them. Sandvoss coins the term 'neu-trosemy' to characterize the 'semiotic condition in which a text allows for so many divergent readings that, intersubjectively, it does not have any mean-ings at all' (p. 126). Thus, the openness of the text in Sandvoss' argument allows the text to become more a part of the identity of the subject and less something that is engaged with reflexively. Fans' involvement with the text is mirror-like. While this has important aspects, there is a danger that contradictory aspects of these processes become subsumed beneath this overarching theory. While this is recognized by this account, there is in my view a danger of psychologiz-ing social processes to a greater extent than is warranted. To develop this point of view, I turn to the work of Couldry.

Place, space and the extended audience

I have argued throughout this book that it is important to conceptualize the relationships between space, social activity and audiences. Couldry has explored these ideas in his work on media, power, and ritual. In his earlier work, he sought, while recognizing the significance of arguments such as those in *Audiences*, to argue that there was a shift away from the adequate study of power. While, I have argued in Chapter 4, these sorts of argument are not to be followed in general, I have suggested that perspectives on power do need to be reformulated to take account of the issues raised in the audiences' text.

In *The Place of Media Power*, Couldry (2000b) theorizes the symbolic power of the media in terms of five processes: framing, ordering, naming, spacing and imagining. The media frame our views of reality, but, more partic-ularly in Couldry's analysis, they 'sustain the frame in which our experiences of the social occur' (p. 178). Another way of thinking this is that the media sustain the scenic constitution of social life that I have argued for previously. Furthermore, in Couldry's view this frame is ordered hierarchically: 'Naming refers to the media's authority as the principal source of social facts' (p. 178). The interconnection between these processes is 'reinforced further by a dimen-sion that is normally hidden: spacing' (p. 178). The media, argues Couldry, are bounded. Borders are erected around the media world that continue to reinforce media power. Certain media places where 'ordinary' people are allowed contact with such spaces of media power seem to open these spaces, but actually they are ultimately controlled by the media institutions and prac-tices. The sites of reality TV and their participants are regulated, as are the visits to media places, such as the Vancouver of *The X-Files*, the sets of series such as *Coronation Street* or the home of Elvis at Graceland.

Finally, Couldry considers imagining, which 'refers to our imaginative and emotional investments in the symbolic hierarchy of the media frame' (p. 178). Thus, in a sophisticated and neo-Durkheimian fashion (see also Couldry 2003 for a consideration of media ritual), Couldry seeks to reconsider the ways in which media power operates – this is 'an abstract way of bringing out the complexities in a process of naturalisation which would otherwise be an undifferentiated object: "media power" ' (p. 179). Thus he argues that his argument has shown 'on the one hand, the increasing thematisation, and public awareness, of the media production process and, on the other hand, the mediatisation, perhaps even spectacularisation, of certain aspects of everyday life' (p. 182). This is an important argument and I now turn to the implications of this retheorization of power for the theory and study of the audience.

Couldry (2005) has used these sorts of argument concerning the nature of power to argue that audiences can be retheorized. He contends that the characterization of contemporary society and culture via the idea of the extended audience has much to recommend it. However, in addition to the concerns that he has about the way in which power is theorized, he also raises concerns about the way in which it is argued that people are becoming both media performers and audience members. However, he tends to treat this idea in a relatively narrow way. That is, while it can be argued that people are performers within the media frame as summarized earlier, this is not quite the same thing as suggesting that they are performers within the institutions of the media. Thus, Couldry tends to slide into a discussion of the specific roles that people have within the media within, for example, TV reality shows and their more informal contacts with the media. There is nothing wrong with this per se; however, the argument that we were making and that I have been discussing in much of this book is itself wider. It is that social and cultural relations in the wider sense are being changed through such processes. However, while this is, I would suggest, an important rider to Couldry's argument, it does not mean that the wider points about the audience are not useful to my approach. Moreover, I have no desire to argue that media corporations do not possess or exercise power, rather that such power has to be theorized in the context of changing relations of ordinary life. In my view this is not the same as arguing that this power is reduced (as Couldry 2005: 196 characterizes our view), but that it has changed, that it is indeed dispersed and that media fragmentation means that the media frame is less consistent than it once was.

On the basis of these criticisms, Couldry argues that the idea of the diffused audience should be replaced by that of the 'extended audience'. He says that:

> The notion of the 'extended' audience requires us to examine the whole spectrum of talk, action and thought that draws on media, or is oriented to media. In this way, we can broaden our understanding of the relationship between media and media audiences as part of our understanding of contemporary media culture.
>
> (Couldry 2005: 196)

This seems perfectly fine to me, but I am unable to agree that the idea of extension fits the bill better than the idea of diffusion. Indeed, my suggestion is that the idea of the extended audience tends to take too much of the baggage of previous theorizations of the media and power with it. Thus, the idea of extension tends to suggest that previous understandings of the audience need to be extended to fit the sorts of new audience situations that Couldry (2005) considers and has addressed in his previous work (2000b, 2003). These include reality TV, the visits to media sets, webcam culture, and so on. While this, on one level, may be seen as a terminological dispute, it does refer to issues of how one can distinguish different audience positions. This is where the distinctions that I began this chapter by repeating are important, as indeed is the further position of the petty producer, because as Couldry suggests:

> Indeed, if the 'ordinary life' of audiences continues to generate revenues for media corporations as it did in the late 1990s and early 2000s, even the boundary between the study of audiences and the study of media production cannot be assumed. For, as we have seen, the worlds of the audience and media production are not sealed off hermetically from each other (see Toynbee 2006), but intersect in what particular audience members do. Each of these 'worlds', after all, is just one aspect of the larger picture of media's role in the social world.
>
> (Couldry 2005: 220)

Thus, the boundaries between a producer and a consumer are subject to some erosion but the particular aspects of these differences still need to be theorized. While Couldry's idea of extension suggests important dimensions that need to be connected to that of diffusion and is therefore important in those terms and for deepening the scope of audience studies in itself, it does not necessarily represent an advance on the idea of diffusion. However, it is significant that this important discussion of the audience in more social terms ends up with a concept of extension in the way that the work examined earlier in the chapter does with respect to the idea of the self.

Enthusing: diffusion and the self

The ideas of the extended audience and the extended self are of significant importance, as they allow consideration of how ideas of the audience and the self need reconsideration in the context of the developed media frame and the impact of commitment to media and cultural forms on the sense of the self. However, as with the idea of the extended audience and previous ideas of the audience, media relations and power, the idea of the extended self seems to remain rather too much on the territory of previous studies of the nature of the self and media. Paradoxically, perhaps, they carry too much baggage from previous understandings of the media and culture. Thus the extended audience idea focuses rather too narrowly on the audience relationship with new and old media and the idea of the extended self and the role of the secondary transitional object likewise keeps too tight a connection between the self and particular and singular objects. Extension seems to convey the idea that what previously existed has simply been extended or built on, rather than transformed through addition into something else. Therefore to capture this, I argue it is important to recognize that the audience is diffused as is the self.

This takes into account the advances of these arguments, but seeks to apply them across a range of different experiences and activities. Importantly, these ideas are concerned with the way in which these experiences are connected to identifications with a range of activities that can become more or less salient to the individual at certain moments. It has been much remarked that in contemporary times, the self has become more pluralistic, and that conceptualizing this as diffused allows examination of the different aspects of identity and how they are salient in different ways and at different times.

My suggestion is that all these aspects of identity have been and are being affected by cultural and social changes, not least those connected to the media. However, this happens in different ways and to varying extents. Thus, while the literature on fandom and media audiencing in the more narrowly conceived sense prompts a number of further understandings, it has limitations.

In the sense that audiencing and performing have changed and diffused, then so too has the self. One way of thinking this is to argue that the diffused self has actually grown to incorporate a greater range of dimensions. This is where the idea of extension of the self is particularly resonant. However, the tendency in such work is to conceive this extension in relation to one main cultural form or experience, be it football, Batman or Elvis Presley, for example. The transitional objects are connected to one of these experiences. However, it can be argued that there is actually a multiplicity of such experiences and forms that are diffusing the self. People have a range of social and cultural activities that they engage with and I suggest that this range is growing as facilitated by consumer experiences. This may mean people moving in and out of activities with some rapidity (see Chapter 7) or becoming more omnivoric (see Chapter 8). It also means that while they become part of the constitution of the diffused self, they are differentially important as part of it. Moreover, enthusiasm for children or parents may be much more significant than that for Elvis Presley, but there are a number of features that such enthusiasms have in common, especially as they have been theorized during the course of this book.

The audience continuum that has been reiterated in this chapter therefore remains of significance in thinking through the different audience positions, within the diffused audience, but also allows consideration of the investment of the self in different activities. This is not simply an abstract typology, but as has been argued is also the basis for a career and levels of personal investment (Crawford 2003, 2004). Hills' (2002) idea of autoethnography captures aspects of one way in which these processes can be considered. The life biography of individuals needs discussion in the context of media-related shifts, but also with respect to a range of other social and cultural changes (Gauntlett and Hill 1999). This sort of method is not simply to be used on the writing subject or more narrowly in a media context. When generalized, it can be an important aspect of how the enthusing and diffused self can be studied in the context of the diffused audience of ordinary life.

10 Conclusions

In the late spring of 2006, I spent parts of four consecutive Saturdays in the following ways: On the first, I went with my wife and our two sons (aged 19 and 12) to see the American singer and guitarist Bonnie 'Prince' Billy perform with the Edinburgh-based Scottish/Irish 'traditional' band Harem Scarem. This happened during the course of a short break in the north of Scotland where we stayed with my parents and visited members of my wife's family and other family members of mine who live nearby. During the visit we did a range of other things, including shopping for food, books and CDs and walking on the beach. The next weekend we celebrated my birthday by going away for the weekend with our closest friends. The weekend in Helsinki included eating out, visiting a contemporary art museum, hearing a salsa band in a jazz club and exploring parts of the city by simply wandering around. The next Saturday evening we attended the birthday party of a friend who lives close by. This took place in a local village hall and involved dancing to music provided by bands involving the friend and her husband. The first part was 'traditional' folk music and the second a 60s' covers band. On the final Saturday we took part in a safari supper organized by neighbours, which involved local friends eating different courses of a meal in different houses and walking around between.

This short account obviously leaves a lot out, such as a number of the more mundane things that I did in between. It thus perhaps makes my life sound rather more exciting and active than it actually is. In between these Saturday events, for instance, I listened to lots of music, read books, devoted much time to television (still the leisure activity that takes up most of our time), went to work, did provision shopping and so on. In addition, many times I spend my Saturday evening cooking and watching programmes like *Doctor Who*, *Strictly Come Dancing*, *The X Factor*, *Match of Day* and *The West Wing* on television. However, the activities on the four consecutive Saturdays of my ordinary life mean rather a lot to me and therefore involve a number of investments in my diffused identity that are important and in that sense extraordinary. Let me just pick out some aspects relative to some of the themes that I have deployed and explored during the course of the book.

First, these Saturdays involved a number of occasions when I was a member of a 'simple' audience such as at the Bonnie 'Prince' Billy concert, seeing the salsa band and watching the 60s' group. Sometimes, this audience activity took on other dimensions when I danced (very badly) to the bands. Sometimes, this involved group activity as when I engaged in organized traditional Scottish country dancing with the folk group at the birthday celebration. Thus even this simple audience activity involved me in performing (I danced badly in front of others, with little shame) and audiencing in the sense that I was an audience for others who were performing in similar ways. Indeed, a significant part of the pleasure of attending the salsa band was seeing the performances of the other dancers, who knew what they were doing to different levels of skill and poise and whose actions were clearly part of the communication and display of their skill. Thus the simple audience rapidly shades into the interaction of diffused audience processes of ordinary life. During this time I was also a member of the mass audience for television on many occasions, mainly engaging in this activity with various members of my family.

Second, there were a number of special occasions here of the type that I have suggested involve greater degrees of performance and display than would have been the case even in fairly recent times. Thus, I can go fairly easily (if I have the money, see later, and if I can overcome my guilt about the planetary effects of increased air travel) to Helsinki from the north of England for a weekend. Indeed, at the airport on a Friday there were lots of groups departing for other cities as part of hen and stag parties, some of then wearing the t-shirts to display to us as audiences that they were doing this. These activities involve rituals like drinking bottles of Champagne or quantities of beer first thing in the morning. Special occasions were being marked with performance, including my birthday and that of our local friend, and marked with a range of performances and audience-like activity.

Third, these activities can be thought of via the different forms of capital: economic, cultural and social. Thus, I need economic capital to engage in a number of these activities. Some are more expensive than others, but they all cost something. This form of capital, like all others, is unevenly distributed and many people could not afford what I have described. I am privileged. The activities also involve cultural capital, thus I deployed this around my appreciation of the music of Bonnie 'Prince' Billy and the contemporary art museum. Finally, all the activities were social and involved networks of different kinds: family (immediate and wider), friends (of different types and longevity) and sometimes people whom I had met for the first time. In different ways, the activities reinforced existing or offered the potential to develop new social ties and networks. Some of these are very deep and intimate, others more passing.

Fourth, the activities are contextualized by wider processes such as globalizing and hybridizing. Travel and connection are easier and I was also able to eat in a Nepalese restaurant in Helsinki (as well as a 'traditional' one), see a salsa band play in a Scandinavian capital city and chat in English in a café queue there with an American and a Finn who had lived in different parts of the world. I saw an American 'alt country' singer play with a Scottish/Irish band in a small community hall in the north of Scotland, on a tour promoted by the Scottish Arts Council to an audience that included 'local' people, those on holiday and those enthusiasts who had travelled some distance.

Fifth, the activities involved interconnected processes of distinguishing and distinction, belonging, individual identity and enthusing. I seek perhaps to distinguish myself from others by things like my appreciation of particular types of art, music and food and write about them here. However, the activities I have described also condense some patterns of elective belonging. I was not born where I live, but part of my feeling of belonging there involves my connections with my family, who live there with me and who attend local schools and have local friends, as well as my interactions with local friends and neighbours. Elective belonging also condenses other aspects of forms of belonging that are important to us in individual ways, such as connections to people (for example, family and friends) and places (in my case, the north of Scotland), which are parts of our senses of self. This also involves things like enthusiasms. My liking for popular music runs through a lot of the activities that I have described and this is an important part of my diffused identity, which often connects it to other aspects of who I am (as a husband, father, son, in-law family member, close friend, acquaintance, neighbour, academic, and so on). The diffused identity is thus network or web-like.

Finally, my actions and activities may involve different degrees of intention and rational action and, indeed, they involve a number of decisions, some much more significant than others. However, they also involve reciprocity, friendship and love in varying degrees. There is a danger that characterizations and theorizations of everyday life of the type that I considered earlier in the book downgrade these aspects of life. This is not always the case and I am definitely not suggesting that we simply *celebrate* ordinary life. However, I am opposed to both the critical and celebratory positions as *a priori*. Moreover, I hold the view that a fully social media and cultural studies needs to recognize the complexity of the interaction of the ordinary and extraordinary and deploy the now many tools that we have to understand its changing nature better. My main hope is that this continues to develop in ways that draws on a range of sources. Thus, in many respects the intervention of this book is to argue for a further shift in the study of the nature of ordinary culture that represents an argument for the merger of two main streams of thought.

My view, therefore, is that, broadly, media and cultural studies' approaches to audiences have become more social as they have progressed and that this is to be welcomed. However, despite the arguments of writers such as Bull (2000), Lembo (2000) and Silverstone (1994) and others who have 'socialized' media and cultural studies, they are still not social enough, in that some important interventions are not deployed in the analysis. By the same token, many aspects of sociological study have been insufficiently cultural, in that (and this is a very crude characterization) they have tended to suggest that modes of social inequality can be considered outside the parameters of the living out of ordinary life. A significant part of my project therefore has been to bring the points where these traditions are proximate ever more closer. This has meant that I have summarized and drawn on for my analysis those forms of the study of media and culture from within the media and cultural studies traditions that have moved closer to the socio-cultural analysis of ordinary life, while retaining a consideration of media and interaction themselves. Contrariwise, there have been moves from within those parts of sociology that have considered modes of inequality to more fully incorporate cultural analysis. In this expanding approach, I have drawn extensively on the works of writers including Devine, Skeggs, Savage and Sayer. In addition, the work in the tradition of North American sociology of culture has much to contribute as have those forms of political science that have addressed overall processes of social and cultural life. Moreover, I have also suggested that there are other forms of analysis that have and are bringing these different aspects of work together in creative ways. Again, in the course of the analysis I have tried to represent what can be seen as exemplars of this evolving mode of analysis in work by such as Crawford, Couldry, Laughey and Sandvoss. In many respects my argument is for a synthesis of the traditions considered here and which can be found with different emphases in the studies discussed here.

In the rest of these conclusions, I summarize the main contours of this approach to ordinary life. I do not simply reiterate the argument for ordinary life, but focus on the overall theoretical approach and the specific dimensions of this that I believe illuminate the processes of ordinary life. My general approach therefore derives from an approach to audience and performance processes, which are seen to have become increasingly important as society has become more media drenched and mediatized. Contemporary ordinary life, therefore, should be theorized in terms of a dynamic of the interaction between performing and audiencing. I have drawn on recent developments in cultural theory to further ground this analysis and do not repeat the way of doing so here.

The basic point is that more social and cultural processes involve performing and audiencing as if in media life and that processes of ordinary life are increasingly revealing these dimensions. I have sought to provide examples of this at points. This also implies a dynamic between the more mundane processes of ordinary life and the more extraordinary moments where ordinary life becomes invested with greater significance (as in enthusing). These are the moments that can be seen as extraordinary. The detail of such a dynamic remains to be further explored. It is important to emphasize that an important part of this argument is that various media have become more significant in ordinary life in providing ways to live through these processes, but also as fuelling them through the resources for imagination, interaction and identity work that they provide. I have also argued that this theorization requires continued attention to forms of social inequality and division and have considered work on class, as a specific example in this light. I do not wish to repeat the specifics of this argument here, but reiterate that I see this as doing what I have suggested earlier, i.e. bringing together an attention to the media with a fuller understanding of the nature of social context and change. Moreover, in this book I have sought to locate that theory in the context of wider processes of social and cultural change. Again, I do not repeat that analysis here. There is, of course, much more to be said about all those processes than I have managed here. That is inevitable, but I hope that enough has been given to show the way in which these different aspects can be shown to interconnect.

I have sought to examine the way in which performing and audiencing operate in an increasingly spectacular society through a focus on broad processes of belonging, distinguishing, individualizing and enthusing and want to use space here to emphasize some of the main points that I have sought to establish through this consideration. Let me begin with the process of distinguishing. Through discussion of a variety of authors, I have drawn on a post-Bourdieu type of analysis of social and cultural distinction. This is significant, as I have suggested in a number of ways, but it is also limited, in two main ways that I have considered in an interconnected fashion. First, there is a danger that all social and cultural processes are seen as fundamentally concerned with distinction or with distinguishing the status of one group from another. Second, there is the issue that these processes are seen as tactics, strategies or rational action towards a goal, when, in fact, they may be more inchoate and diffuse (as are identities). A key aim, therefore, has been both to argue that culture is not simply concerned with strategic or tactical distinction as it moves in messy and complex ways that may indeed be intended and also to imply that there are consequences on a number of fronts. I have used a variety of studies to make these points. It is therefore important to stress that while distinguishing cultures from others and thereby seeking social distinction is an important part of ordinary life, it always operates in contexts that bring in other key processes, which are linked.

Another important process is that of belonging. In many respects belonging is about reassurance that one feels comfortable in a social and cultural situation. However, one of the potential problems with the idea of belonging is that it (like the related idea of community) suggests a degree of fixity. It has often been argued that in a rapidly changing, hypermodern or globalizing world, such fixity is in decline. However, even if this is the case, it can be argued that belonging is still very important as individuals strive for some sense of fixing, but that therefore it needs to be conceptualized in revised ways. It is in this context that I have deployed the concept of elective belonging (Savage et al. 2005) in this book. The power of this concept is that it allows for consideration of the mobility of belonging and opens a clear space for the choices that people make. Moreover, while in much of our discussion of the concept it is theorized through connection to place, that connection is also through a range of social and cultural processes that display both distinction and individuality, which are, in many ways, filtered and condensed through place. However, other dimensions of belonging could represent different starting points for the consideration of patterns of elective behaviour that have alternative dimensions. Thus, for example, family life and choice of partner can be seen to as part of elective belonging. Again I wish to emphasize the way in which a critical part of elective belonging is the performing of identities and the performing of social and cultural activity. As I have emphasized, this is a process that is real and involves multiple audiences. Moreover, the process of elective belonging in a hypermodern world increasingly involves connections via media and connections that are influenced by the performance as if they were mediatized as through the mass media. I have tried to further the study of audience processes through these sorts of route in this book.

Other key processes that I have emphasized are those of individualizing and identity. While the idea of identity has been much considered in recent academic work, the relationship between the individual and the social has been a continued theme of stress in sociology and cultural studies. I have not sought to address that debate in its usual terms in this book. Rather, I have sought to explore ideas of identity and individualization through a number of studies, but would emphasize the importance of the consideration of what I have termed enthusing in this book, again built on earlier analyses. A key strength of recent discussions of fandom, enthusing and audiences such as in the work of Hills (2002), Sandvoss (2005) and Couldry (2005) is precisely this attention to social, cultural and individual processes. Other work on class also has such dimensions (especially Sayer 2005; Skeggs 2004). A key theme in these literatures is the idea that the self is extended via accumulative and media processes. I have on a number of levels sought to follow this idea, but I have taken it in a direction that suggests that this is not just a process of extension but also one that involves processes of diffusion and interconnection. In this sense, the self is produced and reproduced not just through prosthetic processes that involve taking on and taking off aspects of identity and selfhood or the addition of elements, but the constitution and reconstitution of a diffuse and shifting self that is able to perform electively in a wide range of increasingly audienced situations. The term diffusion connects this to the idea of the diffused audience.

In the first chapter of this book, I exemplified the changing nature of media contexts by considering very briefly some of the changes that have occurred over my lifetime and in this conclusion have explored some aspects of my more recent ordinary life. This was done in a spirit of illumination but also to begin the consideration of what I have subsequently termed ordinary life. While this has some dimensions of the kind of autoethnography favoured by Hills (2002), which has become a part of ethnographic and anthropological debate, I mainly seek to try to demonstrate the interconnections between dimensions of a performative and audienced ordinary (with extraordinary features) life and wider social and cultural processes.

I have no doubt that readers of this book could perform the same exercise in ways that illuminate the specific aspects of ordinary life, which are part of wider social and cultural changes. It is very likely that this exercise will reveal the critical significance of a range of different media. I have no doubt that this aspect of ordinary life will continue to grow in significance.

References

Abbott, A. (2001) *Chaos of Disciplines*. Chicago: University of Chicago Press.

Abercrombie, N. and Longhurst, B. (1998) *Audiences: A Sociological Theory of Performance and Imagination*. London: Sage.

Adkins, L. and Skeggs, B. (eds) (2004) *Feminism after Bourdieu*. Oxford: Blackwell.

Ang, I. (1996) *Living Room Wars: Rethinking Media Audiences for a Postmodern World*. London: Routledge.

Anthias, F. (2005) 'Social stratification and social inequality: models of intersectionality and identity', in F. Devine, M. Savage, J. Scott and R. Crompton (eds) *Rethinking Class: Culture, Identities and Lifestyle*. Basingstoke: Palgrave Macmillan.

Appadurai, A. (1993) 'Disjuncture and difference in the global cultural economy', in B. Robins (ed.) *The Phantom Public Sphere*. Minneapolis and London: University of Minnesota Press.

Bacon-Smith, C. (1992) *Enterprising Women: Television Fandom and the Creation of Popular Myth*. Philadelphia: University of Pennsylvania Press.

Bagnall, G., Longhurst, B. and Savage, M. (2003) 'Children, belonging and social capital: the PTA and middle class narratives of social involvement in the north-west of England', *Sociological Research Online*, 8(4).

Barker, M. and Brooks, K. (1998) *Knowing Audiences: Judge Dredd: Its Friends, Fans and Foes*. Luton: University of Luton Press.

Bell, V. (1999a) 'Performativity and belonging: an introduction', in V. Bell (ed.) *Performativity and Belonging*. London: Sage.

Bell, V. (1999b) 'Historical memory, global movements and violence: Paul Gilroy and Arjun Appadurai in conversation', in V. Bell (ed.) *Performativity and Belonging*. London: Sage.

Bennett, A. (2000) *Popular Music and Youth Culture: Music, Identity and Place*. Basingstoke: Macmillian.

Bennett, A. and Peterson, R. A. (eds) (2004) *Music Scenes: Local, Translocal, and Virtual*. Nashville, TN: Vanderbilt University Press.

Bennett, T. and Silva, E. B. (2004) 'Everyday life in contemporary culture', in E. B. Silva and T. Bennett (eds) *Contemporary Culture and Everyday Life*. Durham: Sociology Press.

Bennett, T. and Watson, D. (2002a) 'Understanding everyday life: introduction', in T. Bennett and D. Watson (eds) *Understanding Everyday Life*. Oxford: Blackwell.

Bennett, T. and Watson D. (eds) (2000b) *Understanding Everyday Life*. Oxford: Blackwell.

Berman, M. (1983) *All that is Solid Melts into Air: The Experience of Modernity*. London: Verso.

Berthoud, R. and Gershuny, J. (2000) 'Seven years in the lives of British families', in R. Berthoud and J. Gershuny (eds) *Seven Years in the Lives of British Families: Evidence on the Dynamics of Social Change from the British Household Panel Survey*. Bristol: The Policy Press.

Boden, S. (2003) *Consumerism, Romance and the Wedding Experience*. Basingstoke: Palgrave Macmillan.

Bourdieu, P. (1984) *Distinction: A Social Critique of the Judgement of Taste*. London: Routledge & Kegan Paul.

Bourdieu, P. (1999) *The Weight of the World*. Cambridge: Polity.

Bryson, B. (1996) ' "Anything but heavy metal": symbolic exclusion and musical dislikes', *American Sociological Review*. 61: 884–99.

Bryson, B. (1997) 'What about the univores? Musical dislikes and group-based identity construction among Americans with low levels of education', *Poetics*, 25: 141–56.

Bull, M. (2000) *Sounding Out the City: Personal Stereos and the Management of Everyday Life*. Oxford: Berg.

Bull, M. and Back, L. (eds) (2003) *The Auditory Culture Reader*. Oxford: Berg.

Butler, J. (1993) *Bodies that Matter: On the Discursive Limits of Sex*. London: Routledge.

Butler, J. (1997) *Excitable Speech: A Politics of the Performative*. London: Routledge.

Butler, J. (1999) *Gender Trouble: Feminism and the Subversion of Identity*. London: Routledge (10th anniversary edition).

Carrabine, E. and Longhurst, B. (1999) 'Mosaics of omnivorousness: middle-class youth and popular culture', *New Formations*. 38: 125–40.

Charles, S. (2005) 'Paradoxical individualism: an introduction to the thought of Gilles Lipovetsky', in G. Lipovetsky, *Hypermodern Times*. Cambridge: Polity.

Cohen, S. (1999) 'Scenes', in B. Horner and T. Swiss (eds) *Key Terms in Popular Music and Culture*. Oxford: Blackwell.

Corner, J. (2002) 'Performing the real', *Television and New Media*, 3(3): 255–69.

Couldry, N. (2000a) *Inside Culture: Re-imagining the Method of Cultural Studies*. London: Sage.

Couldry, N. (2000b) *The Place of Media Power: Pilgrims and Witnesses of the Media Age*. London: Routledge.

Couldry, N. (2003) *Media Rituals: A Critical Approach*. London: Routledge.

Couldry, N. (2005) 'The extended audience: scanning the horizon', in M. Gillespie (ed.) *Media Audiences*. Maidenhead: Open University Press in association with The Open University.

Crafts. S. D., Cavicchi, D. and Keil, C. (1993) *My Music*. Hanover and London: Wesleyan University Press, University Press of New England.

Crawford, G. (2003) 'The career of the sport supporter: the case of the Manchester Storm', *Sociology*, 37(2): 219–37.

Crawford, G. (2004) *Consuming Sport: Fans, Sport and Culture*. London: Routledge.

Crompton, R. and Scott, J. (2005) 'Class analysis: beyond the cultural turn', in F. Devine, M. Savage, J. Scott and R. Crompton (eds) *Rethinking Class: Culture, Identities and Lifestyle*. Basingstoke: Palgrave Macmillan.

Crook, S. (1998) 'Minotaurs and other monsters: "everyday life" in recent social theory', *Sociology*, 32(3): 523–40.

DeNora, T. (2000) *Music in Everyday Life*. Cambridge: Cambridge University Press.

DeNora, T. and Belcher, S. (2000) ' "When you're trying something on you picture yourself in a place where they are playing this kind of music": musically sponsored agency in the British clothing retail sector', *Sociological Review*, 48(1), 80–101.

Devine, F. (2004) *Class Practices: How Parents Help Their Children Get Good Jobs*. Cambridge: Cambridge University Press.

Devine, F. and Savage, M. (2005) 'The cultural turn, sociology and class analysis', in F. Devine, M. Savage, J. Scott and R. Crompton (eds) *Rethinking Class: Culture, Identities and Lifestyle*. Basingstoke: Palgrave Macmillan.

Erickson, B. (1996) 'Class, culture and connections', *American Journal of Sociology*, 102(1): 217–51.

Erlmann, V. (ed.) (2004) *Hearing Cultures: Essays on Sound, Listening and Modernity*. Oxford: Berg.

Fortier, A.-M. (2000) *Migrant Belongings*. Oxford: Berg.

Foucault, M. (1979) *Discipline and Punish: The Birth of the Prison*. Harmondsworth: Penguin.

Fowler, B. (2000) 'Introduction', in B. Fowler (ed.) *Reading Bourdieu on Society and Culture*. Oxford: Blackwell.

Gardiner, M. E. (2000) *Critiques of Everyday Life*. London: Routledge.

Garfinkel, H. (1967) *Studies in Ethnomethodology*. Englewood Cliffs, NJ: Prentice Hall.

Gauntlett, D. and Hill, A. (1999) *TV Living: Television, Culture and Everyday Life*. London: Routledge.

Gershuny, J. (2000) *Changing Times: Work and Leisure in Postindustrial Society*. Oxford: Oxford University Press.

Giddens, A. (1990) *The Consequences of Modernity*. Cambridge: Polity.

Goffman, E. (1963) *Behaviour in Public Places: Notes on the Social Organization of Gatherings*. New York: Free Press.

Goffman, E. (1969) *The Presentation of Self in Everyday Life*. Harmondsworth: Penguin.

Goffman, E. (1974) *Frame Analysis*. Garden City, NY: Doubleday.

Grazian, D. (2004) 'The symbolic economy of authenticity in the Chicago blues scene', in A. Bennett and R. A. Peterson (eds) *Music Scenes: Local, Translocal, and Virtual*. Nashville, TN: Vanderbilt University Press.

Gronow, J. and Warde, A. (2001a) 'Introduction', in J. Gronow and A. Warde (eds) *Ordinary Consumption*. London: Routledge.

Gronow, J. and Warde, A. (eds) (2001b) *Ordinary Consumption*. London: Routledge.

Grossberg, L. (1992) *We Gotta Get Out of this Place*. London: Routledge.

Grossberg, L. (1996) 'Identity and cultural studies – is that all there is?', in S. Hall and P. Du Gay (eds) *Questions of Cultural Identity*. London: Sage.

Hall, P. A. (2002) 'Great Britain: the role of government and the distribution of social capital', in R. D. Putnam (ed.) *Democracies in Flux: The Evolution of Social Capital in Contemporary Society*. Oxford: Oxford University Press.

Hall, S. (1980) 'Encoding/decoding', in S. Hall, D. Hobson, A. Lowe and P. Willis (eds) *Culture, Media, Language: Working Papers in Cultural Studies, 1972–79*. London: Hutchinson.

Harrington, C. L. and Bielby, D. D. (1995) *Soap Fans: Pursuing Pleasure and Making Meaning in Everyday Life*. Philadelphia: Temple University Press.

Hesmondhalgh, D. (2002) 'Popular music audiences and everyday life', in D. Hesmondhalgh and K. Negus (eds) *Popular Music Studies*. London: Hodder Arnold.

Hesmondhalgh, D. (2005) 'Subcultures, scenes or tribes? None of the above', *Journal of Youth Studies*, 8(1): 21–40.

Highmore, B. (2002) *Everyday Life and Cultural Theory: An Introduction*. London: Routledge.

Hills, M. (2002) *Fan Cultures*. London: Routledge.

Hills, M. (2005) *How to Do Things with Cultural Theory*. London: Hodder Arnold.

Ho, W.-C. (2003) 'Between globalisation and localisation: a case study of Hong Kong popular music', *Popular Music*, 22(2): 143–57.

Hodkinson, P. (2002) *Goth: Identity, Style and Subculture*. Oxford: Berg.

Holt, D. B. (1995) 'How consumers consume: a typology of consumption practices', *Journal of Consumer Research*, 22: 1–16.

Holt, D. B (1997a) 'Distinction in America: recovering Bourdieu's theory of taste from its critics', *Poetics*, 25: 93–120.

Holt, D. B. (1997b) 'Poststructuralist lifestyle analysis: conceptualizing the social patterning of consumption in postmodernity', *Journal of Consumer Research*, 23: 326–50.

Holt, D. B. (1998) 'Does cultural capital structure American consumption?', *Journal of Consumer Research*. 25: 1–25.

Inglis, D. (2005) *Culture and Everyday Life*. London: Routledge.

Jenkins, H. (1992) *Textual Poachers: Television Fans and Participatory Culture*. London: Routledge.

Kruse, H. (1993) 'Subcultural identity in alternative music culture', *Popular Music*, 12(1): 31–43.

Lash, S. (1990) *Sociology of Postmodernism*. London: Routledge.

Laughey, D. (2006) *Music and Youth Culture*. Edinburgh: Edinburgh University Press.

Lembo, R. (2000) *Thinking Through Television*. Cambridge: Cambridge University Press.

Lin, N. (2001) *Social Capital: A Theory of Social Structure and Action*. Cambridge: Cambridge University Press.

Lipovetsky, G. (1994) *The Empire of Fashion: Dressing Modern Democracy*. Princeton and Oxford: Princeton University Press.

Lipovetsky, G. (2005) *Hypermodern Times*. Cambridge: Polity.

Livingstone, S. (1990) *Making Sense of Television*. London: Pergamon.

Lloyd, M. (1999) 'Performativity, parody, politics', in V. Bell (ed.) *Performativity and Belonging*. London: Sage.

Longhurst, B. (1989) *Karl Mannheim and the Contemporary Sociology of Knowledge*. Basingstoke: Macmillan.

Longhurst, B. (2007) *Popular Music and Society*, 2nd ed. Cambridge: Polity.

Longhurst, B., Bagnall, G. and Savage, M. (2001) 'Ordinary consumption and personal identity: radio and the middle classes in the north west of England', in J. Gronow and A. Warde (eds) *Ordinary Consumption*. London: Routledge.

Longhurst, B., Bagnall, G. and Savage, M. (2004) 'Audiences, museums and the English middle class', *Museum and Society*, 2(2): 104–204.

Longhurst, B., Bagnall, G. and Savage, M. (2007) 'Place, elective belonging and the diffused audience', in J. Gray, C. Sandvoss and C. Lee Harrington (eds) *Fandom: Identities and Communities in a Mediated World*. New York: New York University Press.

Longhurst, B. and Savage, M. (1996) 'Social class, consumption and the influence of Bourdieu: some critical issues', in S. Edgell, K. Hetherington and A. Warde (eds) *Consumption Matters: The Production and Experience of Consumption*. Oxford: Blackwell.

Lury, C. (1998) *Prosthetic Culture: Photography, Memory and Identity*. London: Routledge.

Lyotard, J.-F. (1984) *The Postmodern Condition: A Report on Knowledge*. Manchester: Manchester University Press.

Mannheim, K. (1952) 'The problem of generations', in K. Mannheim, *Essays On the Sociology of Knowledge*. London: Routledge & Kegan Paul.

Mathiesen, T. (1997) 'The viewer society: Michel Foucault's "panopticon" revisited', *Theoretical Criminology*, 1(2): 215–34.

Matthewman, S. and Hoey, D. (2006) 'What happened to postmodernism?', *Sociology*, 40(3): 529–47.

Moores, S. (2000) *Media and Everyday Life in Modern Society*. Edinburgh: Edinburgh University Press.

Moorhouse, H. F. (1991) *Driving Ambitions: An Analysis of the American Hot Rod Enthusiasm.* Manchester: Manchester University Press.

Morley, D. (1980) *The 'Nationwide' Audience.* London: British Film Institute.

Morley, D. (1981) *'The "Nationwide" Audience* – a critical postscript', *Screen Education,* 39: 3–14.

Morley, D. (1986) *Family Television: Cultural Power and Domestic Leisure.* London: Comedia.

Morley, D. (2000) *Home Territories: Media, Mobility and Migrancy.* London: Routledge.

Munro, R. (1996) 'The consumption view of self: extension, exchange and identity', in S. Edgell, K. Hetherington and A. Warde (eds) *Consumption Matters.* Oxford: Blackwell.

Norris, P. (2000) 'The impact of television on civic malaise', in S. J. Pharr and R. D. Putnam (eds) *Disaffected Democracies: What's Troubling the Trilateral Countries.* Princeton: Princeton University Press.

Pahl, R. (1989) 'Is the emperor naked?', *International Journal of Urban and Regional Research,* 13: 711–20.

Penley, C. (1992) 'Feminism, psychoanalysis and the study of popular culture', in L. Grossberg, C. Nelson and P. Treichler (eds) *Cultural Studies.* London: Routledge.

Peterson, R. A. (1990a) 'Why 1955? Explaining the advent of rock music', *Popular Music,* 9: 97–116.

Peterson, R. A. (1990b) 'Audience and industry origins of the crisis in classical music programming: towards world music', in D. B. Pankratz and V. B. Morris (eds) *The Future of the Arts.* New York: Praeger.

Peterson, R. A. (1992) 'Understanding audience segmentation: from elite and mass to omnivore and univore', *Poetics,* 21: 243–58.

Peterson, R. A. (2001) 'Production of culture', *International Encyclopedia of Social Behavioural Science,* 8: 328–32.

Peterson, R. A. and Anand, N. (2004) 'The production of culture perspective', *Annual Review of Sociology,* 30: 311–334.

Peterson, R. A. and Bennett, A. (2004) 'Introducing musical scenes', in A. Bennett and R. A. Peterson (eds) *Music Scenes: Local, Translocal, and Virtual.* Nashville, TN: Vanderbilt University Press.

Peterson, R. A. and Kern, R. (1996) 'Changing highbrow taste: from snob to omnivore', *American Sociological Review,* 61: 900–907.

Peterson, R. A. and Simkus, A. (1992) 'How musical tastes mark occupational status groups', in M. Lamont and M. Fournier (eds) *Cultivating Differences: Symbolic Boundaries and the Making of Inequality.* Chicago: University of Chicago Press.

Pfeil, F. (1990) ' "Makin' flippy-floppy": postmodernism and the baby-boom PMC', in F. Pfeil, *Another Tale to Tell.* London: Verso.

Portes, A. (1998) 'Social capital: its origins and applications in modern sociology', *Annual Review of Sociology,* 24: 1–24.

Probyn, E. (1996) *Outside Belongings.* London: Routledge.

Putnam, R. D. (2000) *Bowling Alone: The Collapse and Revival of American Community.* New York: Simon & Schuster.

Putnam, R. D. and Goss, K. A. (2002) 'Introduction', in R. D. Putnam (ed.) *Democracies in Flux: The Evolution of Social Capital in Contemporary Society.* Oxford: Oxford University Press.

Rodman, G. B. (1996) *Elvis after Elvis: The Posthumous Career of a Living Legend.* London: Routledge.

Rojek, C. (2001) *Celebrity.* London: Reaktion.

Salih, S. (2002) *Judith Butler.* London: Routledge.

Sandvoss, C. (2003) *A Game of Two Halves: Football, Television and Globalization*. London: Routledge.

Sandvoss, C. (2005) *Fans: The Mirror of Consumption*. Cambridge: Polity.

Savage, M., Bagnall, G. and Longhurst, B. (2001) 'Ordinary, ambivalent and defensive: class identities in the north-west of England', *Sociology*, 35(4): 875–92.

Savage, M., Bagnall, G. and Longhurst, B. (2004a) 'Place, belonging and identity: globalisation and the "northern middle class" ', in E. B. Silva and T. Bennett (eds) *Contemporary Culture and Everyday Life*. Durham: Sociology Press.

Savage, M., Bagnall, G. and Longhurst, B. (2004b) 'Local habitus and working-class culture', in F. Devine, M. Savage, J. Scott and R. Crompton (eds) *Rethinking Class: Culture, Identities and Lifestyle*. Basingstoke: Palgrave Macmillan.

Savage, M., Bagnall, G. and Longhurst, B. (2005) *Globalization and Belonging*. London: Sage.

Sayer, A. (2005) *The Moral Significance of Class*. Cambridge: Cambridge University Press.

Schuller, T., Baron, S. and Field, J. (2000) 'Social capital: a review and critique', in S. Baron, J. Field and T. Schuller (eds) *Social Capital: Critical Perspectives*. Oxford: Oxford University Press.

Sennett, R. (1994) 'Foreword', in G. Lipovetsky, *The Empire of Fashion: Dressing Modern Democracy*. Princeton and Oxford: Princeton University Press.

Shank, B. (1994) *Dissonant Identities: The Rock 'n' Roll Scene in Austin, Texas*. Hanover, NH: Wesleyan University Press/University Press of New Hampshire.

Silva, E. and Bennett, T. (eds) (2004) *Contemporary Culture and Everyday Life*. Durham: Sociology Press.

Silverstone, R. (1994) *Television and Everyday Life*. London: Routledge.

Sintas, J. L. and Álvarez, E. G. (2002) 'Omnivores show up again: the segmentation of cultural consumers in Spanish social space', *European Sociological Review*, 18: 353–68.

Skeggs, B. (1997) *Formations of Class and Gender*. London: Sage.

Skeggs, B. (2001) 'The toilet paper: femininity, class and mis-recognition', *Women's Studies International Forum*, 24(3–4): 295–307.

Skeggs, B. (2004) *Class, Self, Culture*. London: Routledge.

Smith, D. E. (1987) *The Everyday World as Problematic*. Milton Keynes: Open University Press.

Smith, G. (2006) *Erving Goffman*. London: Routledge.

Staiger, J. (2005) *Media Reception Studies*. New York: New York University Press.

Stebbins, R. (1992) *Amateurs, Professionals and Serious Leisure*. Montreal: McGill/Queen's University Press.

Strathern, M. (1991) *Partial Connections*. Savage, MD: Rowman & Little.

Strathern, M. (1992) *After Nature: English Kinship in the Late Twentieth Century*. Cambridge: Cambridge University Press.

Straw, W. (1991) 'Systems of articulation, logics of change: communities and scenes in popular music', *Cultural Studies*, 15(3): 368–88.

Straw, W. (2001) 'Scenes and sensibilities', *Public*, 22/23: 245–57.

Straw, W. (2003) 'Scene (location)', in J. Shepherd, D. Horn, D. Laing, P. Oliver and P. Wicke (eds) *Continuum Encyclopedia of Popular Music of the World, Volume 1: Media, Industry and Society*. London: Continuum.

Taylor, T. (1997) *Global Pop: World Music, World Markets*. London: Routledge.

Thomas, L. (2002) *Fans, Feminism and Quality Media*. London: Routledge.

Thompson, E. P. (1961) 'The long revolution parts 1 & 2', *New Left Review*, 9: 24–33 and 10: 34–9.

Tomlinson, J. (1999) *Globalization and Culture*. Cambridge: Polity.

Toynbee, J. (2006) 'The media's view of the audience', in D. Hesmondhalgh (ed.) *Media Production*. Maidenhead: Open University Press.

van Eijck, K. (2000) 'Richard A. Peterson and the culture of consumption', *Poetics*, 28: 207–24.

Warde, A., Martens, L. and Olsen, W. (1999) 'Consumption and the problem of variety: cultural omnivorousness, social distinction and dining out', *Sociology*, 33(1): 105–27.

Warde, A., Tampubolon, G., Longhurst, B., Ray, K., Savage, M. and Tomlinson, M. (2003) 'Trends in social capital: membership of associations in Great Britain, 1991–98', *British Journal of Political Science*, 33: 515–34.

Warde, A., Tomlinson, M. and McMeekin, A. (2000) *Expanding Tastes? Cultural Omnivorousness and Social Change in the UK*. Manchester: CRIC, University of Manchester.

Williams, R. [1958] (1989) 'Culture is ordinary', in R. Williams, *Resources of Hope: Culture, Democracy, Socialism*. London: Verso.

Williams, R. (1960) *Border Country*. London: Chatto & Windus.

Williams, R. [1958] (1963) *Culture and Society: 1780–1950*. Harmondsworth: Penguin.

Williams, R. (1964) *Second Generation*. London: Chatto & Windus.

Williams, R. (1970) *The English Novel from Dickens to Lawrence*. London: Chatto & Windus.

Williams, R. (1979) *The Fight for Manod*. London: Chatto & Windus.

Index

Abbott, A., 63
Abercrombie, N., 9, 10, 28, 37, 44, 52, 106
aerobics, 17
aesthetic evaluation, 72
aestheticization, 18
affective play, 113
age, 98
agency, 39, 89
  structure and, 30–1
alternative rock, 54, 56
amateur production, 56
Anand, N., 92, 97
Anthias, F., 67–8
art world change, 96
associational membership, 6, 82, 84, 85
attachments, 113–14
audience, 4, 5, 6, 9, 119–20
  diffused, 37, 41, 42, 117–18, 119–20
  enthusing *see* enthusing
  extended, 115–17
  fandom *see* fandom
  mass, 36–7, 41, 42, 119–20
  performing and audiencing, 5, 58–60, 68,
    122
  simple, 36, 40–1, 42, 119–20
  spectacle/performance paradigm, 35–48,
    51
  spectacularizing and performing, 28–9
audience continuum, 42–4, 104, 110
Austin, Texas, 52–3, 57
autoethnography, 114, 118

Bagnall, G., 101
behavioural paradigm, 35–6, 51
behaviourism, 106
Bell, V., 38, 39–40

belonging, 5, 45, 67, 121, 123
  elective *see* elective belonging
  local, 24–5, 49–51
Benjamin, W., 10
Bennett, A., 53–4
Bennett, T., 7, 10, 11, 30
Berthoud, R., 77
Blair, T., 97
body, 17
bonding social capital, 32, 81–2
books, 2
border country, 14
Bourdieu, P., 30–1, 49, 64–6, 86, 87
  and fandom, 111
bridging social capital, 32, 81–2
British Film Institute (BFI) tracking study,
    77–81
British Household Panel Survey (BHPS), 77,
    84–5
Bryson, B., 97
Bull, M., 7, 18–19
Butler, J., 38–40, 51

Cameron, D., 96–7
Cantopop, 24
capitalism, 8
capitals, 6, 31, 68, 74–89, 120
  class and education, 85–8
  and fandom, 111
  social capital *see* social capital
Carlisle, 60
Carrabine, E., 101
ceremony, 41
change, 4–5, 5–6, 22–34
  enthusing, 30–4
  globalizing and hybridizing, 22–5

modernity, fragmentation and personal
choice, 25–8
spectacularizing and performing, 28–9
charitable endeavour, 82
Charles, S., 26
Chorlton, Manchester, 101
class, 5, 20–1, 62–73
and education, 85–8
inscription, exchange, value and perspective, 69–71
middle class *see* middle class
morality, evaluation and ordinary life,
71–3
new agenda for culture, identity and,
63–9
responses to, 73
structure and social capital, 83, 84–5
working class, 65–6, 94–5
clubbers, 46
cognitive psychology, 106
Cohen, S., 55, 56–7, 59
commercialization of culture, 12
community, 12–13, 13–14
football fandom, 108–9
imagined communities, 108
scene and, 54
computers, 2
conflict theory, 106
connecting *see* capitals; omnivore thesis;
time use
consumer, 42, 44
and producer of culture, 55–6, 117
consumption, 15, 75–6
context, 100
cosmopolitanism, 56, 58, 101
Couldry, N., 7, 13–15, 41–2, 105, 115–17
'Coventry' scene, 57
Crafts, S.D., 16
Crawford, G., 28, 40–1, 41–2, 44, 107
creativity, cultural, 12, 13
critical Marxism, 8
Crook, S., 7
cultists, 43, 44, 110, 112
cultural capital, 31, 32–3, 120
class, education and, 85–8
cultural creativity, 12, 13
cultural elitism, 12
cultural globalization, 22–4
cultural taste, 93–7
qualitative consideration and modes of
speech, 100–2
see also omnivore thesis

days, time use across, 76–81
DeNora, T., 7, 16–17
Devine, F., 63–6, 75, 85–8, 111
diffused audiences, 37, 41, 42, 117–18,
119–20
diffused self, 117–18, 124
distinction, 111, 121, 123
distinguishing, 5, 6, 121, 123
see also capitals; omnivore thesis; time use
documentary, 29
drag, 51
drifters, 46
dynamism of culture, 12, 13

economic capital, 31, 120
class, education and, 85–8
economic globalization, 22–4
education, 31, 83, 89, 95
class and, 85–8
elective belonging, 49–61, 68, 89, 121, 123
globalizing, 51–2
scene and, 52–8, 112
scene, performing, audiencing and, 58–60
elite-to-mass theory, 93–5
enthusiasts, 43, 44, 110, 112
enthusing, 5, 6, 30–4, 104–18, 121, 124
diffusion and the self, 117–18
place, space and the extended audience,
115–17
reception and sport, 105–9
theories of fandom, 110–15
evaluation, 69–73
inscription, exchange and perspective,
69–71
morality and ordinary life, 71–3
everyday life, 7, 8–11
see also ordinary life
exchange, 69–71
exchangers, 46
extended audience, 115–17
extended self, 117, 124

family, 3
fandom, 6, 33–4, 104–18
audience continuum, 42–4, 104, 110
reception and sport, 105–9
theories of, 110–15
see also enthusing
fashion, 26
feelings, music and, 16–17
feminist theory, 11
fields, 31, 65

film, 1–2, 55–6
fluidity, 64–5
football, 106–9, 110
football stadia, 108–9
formal social capital, 81–2
Foucault, M., 28–9
fragmentation, 5–6, 81, 90–1
    modernity and personal choice,
        25–8
    see also omnivore thesis
framing, 115
Freudian theories of fandom, 114
friendship, 121
functionalism, 106

Gardiner, M.E., 10, 11
Gauntlett, D., 77–81, 89
gender
    and paid and unpaid work, 75–6
    performativity, identity and, 38–9
    and social capital, 83, 85
    and television viewing, 79, 80
generational effects, 82
generational politics, 96
Gershuny, J., 75–7
Giddens, A., 9
globalization, 5, 6, 22–5, 120
    and belonging, 51–2, 57
    football fandom, place and, 108–9
Goffman, E., 10
Goldthorpe, J., 86
Goss, K.A., 81–2
Goth, 53, 54
government actions, 83
Graceland, 112
Grateful Dead, 54
Grazian, D., 54
Gronow, J., 15
Grossberg, L., 12–13, 113

habitus, 30–1, 65, 72
Hall, P.A., 82–4
Hesmondhalgh, D., 57–8
high culture, 93, 95
    see also elite-to-mass theory
Highmore, B., 10–11
Hill, A., 77–81, 89
Hills, M., 44, 110, 111, 113–14
Ho, W.-C., 24
Hodkinson, P., 52, 53, 54
Holt, D.B., 100
Hong Kong pop, 24

human needs, real, 8
hybridization, 5, 6, 22–5, 120
hypermodernity, 26–7, 34

identity, 6, 45, 121, 123–4
    class, culture and, 62–73
    football fandom and, 107–9
    music and construction of, 16–17
    performative enactment, 38–9
    scene and, 59–60
    studies of fandom, 113–14
    television and, 78, 80
    see also self
imagined communities, 108
imagining, 115
incorporation/resistance paradigm (IRP), 9,
        36, 40, 51
individualization, 5, 14–15, 123–4
    modernity, fragmentation and personal
        choice, 25–8
informal social capital, 81–2
informal sociability, 82
Inglis, D., 11
inscription, 69–71
interaction, music and, 16–17
interactionist sociology, 9–10
internet, 54
intersectionality model of social divisions,
        67–8
intimacy, 58
inward-looking social capital, 81–2
iPod, 2, 19

Jenkins, H., 106

Kern, R., 27, 95–7
Kleinian theories of fandom, 114
Kruse, H., 54

Laughey, D., 45–6, 60
lay normativity, 72
leisure time, 75–6
Lembo, R., 46–8
life stages, 77–81, 88
life transitions, 78
Lin, N., 31
Lipovetsky, G., 26–7, 34
Lloyd, M., 39
local belonging, 24–5, 49–51
local scenes, 53
localization, 6
long-run trends, 76–81, 88

Longhurst, B., 9, 10, 20, 28, 37, 44, 52, 99, 101, 106
love, 121
Lyotard, J.-F., 25

magazines, 2, 98
Manchester, 60, 101
Marxism, critical, 8
mass audiences, 36–7, 41, 42, 119–20
mass culture, 93–5
mass observation, 11, 29
Mathiesen, T., 28–9
meanings, personal, 78
media
  defining, 3
  increased importance, 1–3
  use, 20–1
  see also under individual media
media drenching, 3, 5, 10, 102–3
middle class, 20–1, 27, 85, 91
  cultural taste and modes of speech, 101–2
  and education, 85–8
middlebrow culture, 93
mobility, 14, 66, 69
  social mobility, 86–7, 95, 98
modernity, 25–8
modes of speech, 100–2
moral sentiments, 72–3
morality, 71–3
music, 2, 96, 110
  globalization and hybridization, 24
  occupational groups and, 93–4
  omnivorous refrain, 101
  scene, 52–4, 55, 56–7, 57–8, 59, 60
  sound, ordinary life and, 16–19
  univores, 97
  world music, 98–9, 100
  youth subculture, 45–6

naming, 115
narcissism, 18
narrative
  construction by personal stereo users, 18
  of location, 67–8
  scene and, 54–5, 57, 59
needs, real human, 8
networks, 14, 32
  see also social capital
neutrosemy, 115
news consumption, 78
newspapers, 2, 98
Norris, P., 33, 78

occupational groups, 93–5
older people, 79
omnivore thesis, 6, 27–8, 66, 90–103
  early statements and key themes, 92–7
  qualitative consideration and modes of speech, 100–2
  wider applications and development of explanations, 97–9
ordering, 17, 115
  of time and activity, 88–9
ordinary life, 3–4, 5, 7–21, 121–2
  morality, evaluation and, 71–3
  music, sound and, 16–19
  ordering, 88–9
  television viewing and, 78
  theories of everyday life, 7, 8–11
outward-looking social capital, 81–2

paid work, 75–6
panopticism, 29
paradoxical modernity, 26–7
performance, 4, 6, 50
  ordinary life and, 5, 10, 28–9
  spectacle/performance paradigm *see* spectacle/performance paradigm
performative evaluation, 72
performativity, 35–42, 50
performing, 5, 68, 120, 122
  and belonging, 50–1, 58–60
personal choice, 25–8
personal stereos, 18–19
perspective, 69–71
Peterson, R.A., 27, 53–4, 92–7
petty producer, 43–4, 117
photography, 56
place
  and belonging, 51–2, 60
  and extended audience, 115–17
  fandom and, 108–9, 111–12
  and scene, 54, 56–7
political globalization, 22–4
political participation, 83, 84–5
political science, 4
political trust, 83, 85
positionality, 67–8
postmodernism, 5–6, 76, 90–1, 102
  fragmentation and personal choice, 25–8
power, 9, 29, 41–2
  extended audience, 115–17
practice, 30–1
  need to explore practices, 100
Presley, Elvis, 112

producer of culture, 43–4, 55–6, 117
production of culture thesis, 92–3
prosthetic self, 70–1
psychoanalysis, 106, 114
psychological theories of fandom, 114
Putnam, R.D., 4, 31–3, 78, 81–2

racialization, 40
radio, 2
rational action model (RAT), 63, 68, 86
real human needs, 8
reception studies, 105–6
reciprocity, 32, 121
reflexivity, 65
relational nature of identity, 65
repetitiveness, 13, 18–19
residence, 3, 51–2
resistance, 8–9
    incorporation/resistance paradigm, 9, 36,
        40, 51
    and television, 80, 101
resources, 85–8
    see also capitals
retired people, 79
Rodman, G.B., 112
routine, 13, 18–19

Salih, S., 38, 39
Sandvoss, C., 33–4, 43, 107–9, 110, 111–12,
    114, 115
Savage, M., 49–50, 57, 60, 63–6, 77, 99, 101
Sayer, A., 63, 71–3, 102
scene, 52–8, 61, 112
    and narrative, 54–5, 57, 59
    performing, audiencing and elective
        belonging, 58–60
    place and, 54, 56–7
    problems with, 57–8
secondary transitional objects, 113
self
    diffused, 117–18, 124
    extended, 117, 124
    prosthetic, 70–1
    see also identity
self-reflection, 43
Shank, B., 52–3, 57, 58
Silva, E.B., 7, 11, 30
Silverstone, R., 8–9
Simkus, A., 27, 93–4
Simmel, G., 10
simple audiences, 36, 40–1, 42,
    119–20

Skeggs, B., 63, 65–6, 68–71, 101–2
Smith, D.E., 11
social capital, 4, 26–7, 30–3, 88, 120
    in Britain, 81–5
    class, education and, 85–8
social globalization, 22–4
social life, as a game, 68
social mobility, 86–7, 95, 98
social trust, 32, 82–4, 85
sociology, 4
sound, 3, 16–19
space
    and extended audience, 115–17
    fandom and, 108–9, 111–12
    personal stereos and creating, 18
spacing, 115
special days/events, 37, 120
specificities, 100
spectacle, 5, 6, 28–9, 35–42
spectacle/performance paradigm (SPP),
    35–48, 51
    audience positions, 42–4
    research questions, 44–8
speech, modes of, 100–2
sport
    contemporary football, 106–9, 110
    events, 28, 42
Staiger, J., 105–6
status, 27, 76
status group politics, 96–7
Stebbins, R., 44
Straw, W., 52–3, 55, 56, 58
structural change, 96
structuration, 9
structure
    and agency, 30–1
    structuring television viewing, 80
structure-culture-action (S-C-A) approach,
    63–4
subjectivity, 113–14
surfers, 46
surrealism, 10–11
surveillance, 28–9
symbolic capital, 31
synopticism, 29

taste, cultural see cultural taste
telephone, 2
television, 1–2, 9, 33, 55–6
    BFI tracking study, 77–81
    and football fandom, 109
    modes of speech, 101

sociality of television viewing, 46–7
   resistance and, 80, 101
texts, 114–15
thick social capital, 81–2
thin social capital, 81–2
Thompson, E.P., 14
time use, 74, 75–81, 88–9
Tomlinson, J., 22, 23, 25
transitional objects, 113
translocal scenes, 53–4
trust
   political, 83, 85
   social, 32, 82–4, 85

unicity, 23
univores, 27, 94–7
unpaid work, 75–6

value, 69–71
value change, 96

van Eijck, K., 98–9
video technology, 79
violence, television, 79–80
virtual scenes, 53–4
voluntarism, 68, 71
voluntary association membership, 6, 82,
   84, 85

Warde, A., 15, 84–5, 99
Watson, D., 10, 11
way of life, culture as, 12
Williams, R., 7, 12–14, 54
Winnicott, D.W., 113, 114
work, 3
   paid, unpaid and time use,
     75–6
working class, 65–6, 94–5
world music, 98–9, 100

youth subculture, 45–6